Elizabeth Stuart
end, Kent. The
and a Catholic r
ant, ecumenica
became attract
theology and w
lege, Oxford. On gaining a first class degree,
she was awarded the Yates Senior Scholarship
in Theology from St Hugh's College, Oxford,
and moved there to undertake her research
work. She gained her D.Phil. in 1988. She
currently lectures in theology at the College
of St Mark and St John in Plymouth, where
she is particularly involved in teaching
Church History and Political Theology. She
has published a number of articles on Angli-
can/Roman Catholic relations in the nine-
teenth century and on general theological
topics.

THROUGH BROKENNESS

How God Saves Humanity
Through Grace and the
Sacraments

ELIZABETH STUART

Collins
FOUNT PAPERBACKS

This book is dedicated to
my parents, Neil and Vera Stuart;
my sister and brother-in-law,
Veronica and Alan Donaldson,
and to Jane Robson,
with my love

First published in Great Britain by
Fount Paperbacks, London in 1990

Copyright © Elizabeth Stuart 1990

Printed and bound in Great Britain by
William Collins Sons & Co. Ltd, Glasgow

Phototypeset by Input Typesetting Ltd, London

ACKNOWLEDGEMENTS

Thanks are due to Collins for their interest, advice and encouragement, the editors of *Christian* for publishing the three articles out of which this book has grown and for giving me permission to reproduce material from the articles in this book, to Jane Robson for reading the book at every stage of its development and offering incisive criticisms and suggestions for improvement, to my friend Dr Jim Little for sharing brokenness and wholeness, to my colleagues in the Religious Studies and Philosophy Department at the College of St Mark and St John, Plymouth, for their inspiration and encouragement, to all my students for keeping me on my theological toes and teaching me so much, and last, but by no means least, to the Revd Dr Anthony Phillips for teaching me that being a Christian involves "radical discipleship".

My thanks too to Faber & Faber for the extract from T. S. Eliot's *Burnt Norton*, and to Darton, Longman and Todd for the passages from Jean Vanier's *The Broken Body*. All biblical quotations are taken from the Revised Standard Version of the Bible, copyrighted 1946, 1952, © 1971, 1973 by the Division of Christian Education of the National Council of the Churches of Christ in the USA, and used by permission.

CONTENTS

INTRODUCTION

This book began life as a lecture that I was asked to give as part of an adult education course on Pastoral Theology. The topic of the lecture was "grace and the sacraments". As a theologian my immediate instinct was to go straight to the "Doctor of Grace", St Augustine, and discourse learnedly upon the difference between prevenient and subsequent grace, and then to turn to Aquinas on the sacraments and examine his famous theology of the eucharist, depending upon the Aristotelian distinction between substance and accidents. Fortunately it did not take too long for me to wake up to the fact that the people to whom I would be talking would simply not be interested in such theological hairsplitting. They were people who, either in their professional or private lives, had to deal with men and women battered and broken by life, and what they wanted from me was to know whether Christianity had anything to offer the broken and, if it did, how the sacraments convey this. At the time I was feeling pretty battered by life myself. I was in a great deal of physical pain and consequent mental distress, and so the quest to answer the questions which I believed were being put to me became a personal rather than a purely academic one.

This book is a fuller version of the sketchy answer I gave first in my lecture and later developed into three articles which appeared in *Christian* in November 1988, January and May 1989. Early on in my quest I realized that we are all broken by being human, even though we may not acknowledge or realize it. Brokenness is, therefore, a very personal thing but also a shared experience and so I have tried to draw heavily upon my own personal experience of brokenness and wholeness and upon that of others, in the hope that the reader will be able to identify if not with the circumstances then at least with the emotions and reactions.

> *Question*: What meanest thou by this word *Sacrament*?
> *Answer*: I mean an outward and visible sign of an inward and spiritual grace.[1]

This definition of a sacrament will be familiar to millions of Christians. Every day, throughout the world, Christians from almost every tradition will be found participating in one of the sacraments. This book attempts to explore exactly what a sacrament is and what is meant by "grace".

Since the Church has traditionally taught that the sacraments mediate salvation the book begins with a look at the human condition in order to determine exactly what we need saving from. It is argued that to be human is to be broken, that is, to be divided against oneself and one's neighbour and always trying to deny, suppress and escape from parts of ourselves that we find undesirable – our shadow side. Human brokenness manifests itself in our relationships, with ourselves, with others and with God, and in our physical condition. A recurrent charge in this book is that the Church has often been a cause of brokenness rather than a mediator of wholeness. This is a fact that has to be acknowledged. It is not a very surprising fact because the Church consists of human beings who are themselves broken but it is a matter for shame and sorrow because the Church claims to be the body of Christ on earth and is called by him to mediate love, liberation and wholeness, not judgement, imprisonment and brokenness. The Church needs to keep an eye on itself and be aware of its constant need to repent – to turn away from brokenness to wholeness.

Chapter two attempts to show that God offers humanity healing and wholeness through his son, Jesus Christ. A strong and unorthodox incarnationalist view is taken and I argue that God became human in Jesus fully and unconditionally and therefore must have experienced all the pain, alienation and brokenness that being human involves, *including sin and real death*. Out of this utter brokennness God raised Jesus to a new, healed, whole, unalienated existence and revealed that this is what he offers to all humanity. It is this offer that is "grace". An examination of Jesus' earthly ministry reveals that he was devoted to bringing a foretaste of complete wholeness to those who acknowledged their brokenness. It was those who could not face their own brokenness who found themselves threatened by Jesus.

Chapter three endeavours to demonstrate that it is through God's grace that we who stand two thousand years away from the historical Jesus can participate in Christ's resurrection and experience wholeness, however temporarily, in our own lives. This grace is mediated through sacraments, finite realities that convey something of the infinite to individuals or groups. I argue that almost anything can be sacramental and note that this can be particularly true of relationships.

Chapter four looks at those Christian rites which have been designated "sacraments" by the Church. The history of the sacraments is briefly explained and the value of symbol as a sign and mediation of grace explored. The two "dominical" sacraments of baptism and the eucharist are examined in detail and the means by which healing is mediated through them discussed.

In the concluding chapter I argue that the time has come to develop more sacraments to mediate grace to people in particularly important and difficult circumstances that did not exist when the traditional sacraments were developed and fixed.

Unlike most works on grace and the sacraments this book has not been written for academic theologians and canon lawyers. It is written for those "on the ground", those who are dealing with brokenness all around them and who want to make some sense of it by reference to Christ and the Church but who are not seeking easy answers. It is written for those who want to find Christ in brokenness and experience his healing love in the midst of the pain and despair of being human. It is written for those who long to respond to the divine invitation:

> Ho, every one who thirsts, come to the waters;
> and he who has no money, come, buy and eat!
> Come, buy wine and milk without money and
>   without price.
> Why do you spend your money for that which is
>   not bread,
> and your labour for that which does not satisfy?
> Hearken diligently to me, and eat what is good,
>   and
> delight yourselves in fatness. Isaiah 55:1–2

1

Broken Humanity

Yesterday I was accompanied to Mass by a friend. It was the third Sunday of Lent and the theme of the sermon was the need both to express sorrow and hear words of forgiveness. The priest illustrated this point with a story of a child who whilst attending her best friend's birthday party accidentally breaks her friend's favourite present. The child begs forgiveness and becomes distraught when her friend refuses to pronounce the words of forgiveness. After Mass Hilary revealed that she had been deeply moved, not so much by the theme of the sermon as by the story the priest had told. Hilary is still trying to get over the break-up of a relationship that she had hoped and expected would lead to a life-long commitment. Listening to the sermon she realized that she had given to her prospective partner the most precious gift of all – herself. But he had rejected the gift. The act of rejection had, in her own words, broken her. Her friend had recently contacted her asking for forgiveness but Hilary was finding it difficult to find the strength to forgive him for the pain and brokenness he had caused. Whilst telling me all this Hilary became very distressed. "What do you do?", she wept. "If you are going to live you are going to love and if you are going to love you are going to be hurt and broken."

To be human is to be broken. It is to be unwhole and unsound. It is to be a mass of contradictions. It is to be divided against yourself and your neighbour. It is to be always trying to deny, suppress and escape from parts of ourselves that we and those around us brand evil, undesirable, odd or perverted. It is to be constantly trying to hide our weakness, hurt and vulnerability – our shadow side.

Our brokenness manifests itself in various ways and in every aspect of our lives: in our relationships both with ourselves and with others; in our physical condition; and in our relationship with God.

Me and My Shadow

If we are honest most of us would admit to not liking ourselves very much. Everyone has parts of themselves that they dislike, are ashamed of or even find revolting. We all have memories of past experiences that have left us hurt and vulnerable. For the greater part of our lives we suppress these parts of ourselves, banish them from our consciousness and pretend they do not exist. However, we constantly live in fear of others penetrating beneath the surface, beneath the "mask" we assume to the rest of the world, and exposing our shadow side. So we are careful to keep most people at arm's length, far enough away to prevent any threat. We take a lot of trouble over the fashioning of our masks. The clothes we wear are carefully chosen to present a certain image, make the right sort of impression on those with whom we come into contact. Similarly, we adopt attitudes in the company of others which we hope will be taken to be our real nature. We are very careful to disclose only certain amounts of information about ourselves. Our opinions, attitudes and past experiences are all rigorously censored in conversation. Some of us hide behind a mask of apparent openness and spontaneity. We happily tell complete strangers a great deal about ourselves, perhaps even intimate details so we are classed in the minds of others as "open" and "honest". This is the image we want to present. Behind this mask we might be desperately lonely and confused about ourselves. Yet we are perversely fascinated by the masks others assume and we enjoy nothing so much as penetrating them, revealing the people as in some way unacceptable or inferior. Think of a party. Even though you may be feeling tired, fed up or ill you "put on a face" and pretend to be having a wonderful time. Think of all the friendly questions, trivial conversations and witty remarks that characterize a party. It is like a game in which the players flutter round each other revealing just enough of themselves to preserve their own mask whilst at the same time enticing others to expose themselves as fools, as inferiors, as unacceptable. We do this for the purposes of one-upmanship, to establish ourselves in positions of superiority.

In the book of Genesis we are told that, having

eaten fruit from the forbidden tree, Adam and Eve suddenly became self-conscious:

> Then the eyes of both were opened, and they knew that they were naked; and they sewed fig leaves together and made themselves aprons.
>
> Genesis 3:7

Adam and Eve realized what they were truly like and were ashamed so they tried to hide from God behind fig leaves and trees. Like them we hide ourselves behind carefully constructed masks and try to lose ourselves in the company of others. Life can be one long masked ball.

The construction of a personality mask is often a totally unconscious act. Indeed, many people will be reluctant to admit to having a shadow side that needs hiding. We often fool ourselves better than we fool others. Certainly we are not wholly responsible for our shadow side, just as we are not wholly responsible for the creation of our complete personality. A number of forces work together in our formation. To name but a few: hereditary factors; the influence of parents or those responsible for bringing us up; the circumstances in which our formative years are lived; the influence and expectations of society. But whilst the shadow side exists, whether acknowledged or not, a person is unwhole and broken; and without acknowledgement there is no hope of repair.

It is difficult for those who acknowledge their shadow side to resist becoming totally obsessed by their own vulnerability or eaten up by guilt and disgust with those parts of themselves they are ashamed of. Some might resort to drugs, alcohol or other addictive behaviour in order to escape the stifling fog of guilt that surrounds them. Others might throw themselves into a series of intense but doomed relationships in a frantic search for assurance and love. Others might abandon intolerable reality for a life based upon fantasy.

Who creates our shadow side? What dictates which parts of ourselves are acceptable or not? The obvious answer is the society in which we live. The family, the Government, the media and our friends all have very clear ideas about what is and what is not acceptable. What these ideas are based upon is much harder to establish: historical precedent, natural law, the collective unconscious, the folk attitudes of particular societies and classes and, of course, religion. Despite the fact that western society is becoming increasingly secular the so-called "Christian ethic" still provides the basis for much public opinion on what is and what is not acceptable behaviour or what is or what is not correct thinking.

Christianity has a lot to answer for. Despite Christ's command to "love your neighbour *as yourself*" (Mark 12:31), the Church has not encouraged love of self. Whereas Jesus preached unconditional forgiveness, accepted and loved people as they were and was more concerned with what was right with them than with their flaws, his Church very quickly started doing the exact opposite in his name. The Church urged Christians to hate and suppress large areas of themselves, for example, their bodily needs, sexuality, reason, ambition and so on, for the good of their souls.

19

Lists of sins of various grades of severity were issued to help the soul escape from the prison house of humanity. The Church also kindly provided an appropriate set of punishments to help train the Christian to resist temptation. Introspection and self-disgust were encouraged. Those who refused to recognize their sinfulness and repent were obviously beyond the love of God and destined for eternal damnation. If haranguing or persecution did not bring them to their senses they were to be shunned and despised. Only in the second half of the twentieth century has the Church begun to question this approach but the "sin and sinner" mentality still lingers on in both the Church and our so-called tolerant society. Hate your neighbour as you hate yourself but pretend to love him in order to convert him. This, rather than the "great commandment", is the maxim by which the Church and Christian society have lived down the centuries.

I met Sam at university. Sam was not a believer in God but he had been brought up a Christian by church-going Church of England parents. He was bright, very friendly and absolutely charming. He was also one of the most sexually promiscuous people I have ever come across. He made friendships easily and swiftly, treated each person as if she was the most interesting and beautiful woman he had ever met and established a sexual relationship with her. Often he would be sexually involved with several women at a time. But the moment one of his partners tried to elicit some sort of commitment from him he would withdraw from the relationship. There was nothing he hated more than an emotional scene. Life was to be enjoyed; sex and companionship were part of that enjoyment; anything "heavy" that might spoil the fun was to be avoided. At the same time Sam was frightened of rejection and even when he had ended sexual relationships he would not leave his partners alone and would insist that they remain "friends".

As I got to know Sam I became increasingly puzzled as to how someone who apparently had so much going for him and who had chosen to study modern literature, which is nothing if not "heavy", could be content with simply skimming along life's surface and never getting "involved". Eventually all became clear. Sam was wrestling with homosexual inclinations. Some years before I met him Sam had worked abroad and much to his surprise had fallen for a young man and established a sexual and emotional partnership with him. The affair did not last but ended amicably.

On returning to England Sam became very confused about his sexuality. He realized that homosexuality had been part of his nature for a long time and he became increasingly aware of being attracted to men. But he knew his parents dismissed homosexual behaviour as "unnatural", "perverted" and "sinful", and he suspected that most of his friends would react in much the same way. Indeed, he had subscribed to society's view of homosexuality himself. Sam could not cope with both demands at the same time. He thought that he would be rejected by those he loved and respected if he opted for a homosexual lifestyle. Nor could Sam shake off his belief that homosexual behaviour was sinful, even though he professed to be

21

an atheist. Rather than tackle his dilemma honestly Sam chose to repress his homosexual inclinations and keep his shadow side a closely guarded secret. He felt he had to prove to himself and others that he was fully heterosexual and yet he was frightened of letting anyone get too close to him lest his mask crack and reveal his true "dirty" self. Sam spent many years loving and leaving young ladies (with occasional forays into the "gay" scene), causing them much pain and heartbreak and refusing to allow them the time and space to heal and get over their relationship. His women friends wanted him to be straight and his gay friends wanted him to be gay. All the time he was insulating himself from hurt, rejection and need. He thought he was happy, he came to believe in his own mask but beneath the surface he was a broken and confused mess.

In a sense Sam was lucky, he did not have the added burden of being a practising religious person. There are many like Sam who believe that the God whom they love and try to serve hates their true nature and demands that they suppress it and repent of it and expects them to live lonely, unfulfilled lives, deprived of the opportunity of reaching out in love, of giving themselves body and soul to another person and experiencing the deep contentment, fulfilment and creativity of a committed sexual relationship. This is certainly the position adopted by the authorities of most Christian denominations. The theologian Harry Williams painted a vivid picture of the pain involved in being both a Christian and a homosexual in his autobiography:

... this God of mine forbade me to be three-quarters of what I was. He demanded that whole areas of myself should be put in the deep freeze and left there frozen and, with luck, forgotten.

He demanded this of my sexual potential. The elimination of sex was one of the most important clauses in the contract I had made with him ... Even mildly attractive people God regarded as his sexual rivals. He was not a jealous God for nothing. And since sex and emotion are so closely bound up together, God wanted me to be an emotional dwarf so that I might give my stunted heart wholly to him.[1]

The Church inflicts such guilt and misery on many confused and troubled minds – among them, divorcees who crave a second chance fortified by the rites of the Church, women driven to abortion clinics by poverty, shame, confusion, a sense of powerlessness or despair, and women who feel called by God to a priestly ministry in the Church. Though claiming to save, the Church often breaks and batters. It is so easy to brand as "sinners" difficult people, people who dissent and who do not conform to society's norm, and to offer repentance as a panacea. It is so much more difficult to abandon the rule book as Jesus did and treat everyone as a person with a right to dignity, a right to be listened to, a right to be loved and cared for, to be respected, to be accepted as they are and not to be judged. This approach is so difficult because it is so costly. It requires personal involvement. Prejudice and "face" must be put aside and people who do not love themselves must be shown that God loves them. It involves reaching out to some very unsavoury characters: adulterers, addicts, murderers, rapists, child abusers, embezzlers, the homeless and worthless, criminals and perverts of every hue, reaching out and embracing with love, not battering with Bibles. And it involves risk, the risk of being rejected.

Society has its own special list of "sinners", people it hates because they rock the boat and raise questions about the value and moral character of the society in which they live. These people are the "failures", the ones who have not made it, who have not benefited materially from the way society is run. These are the people who do not think the society they are in is full of opportunity, wealth, happiness, tolerance and care, at least not for them. These are the homeless, the unemployed, the poverty-stricken elderly, the single-parents, the chronically sick, the broken families, the delinquents, the criminals, the ones who have been "found out". It is so much easier for society to heap the blame for failure back on to the shoulders of these already broken people than to own up to its own responsibility and to set about healing them. So it brands them as "lazy", "unable to manage money", "out for what they can get", or it blames their condition on the moral bankruptcy of their parents. What is more, society is staunchly unforgiving: misdemeanours or more serious "wrongdoing" will never be forgotten but will haunt the sinner forever, blocking new paths and clouding the vision of potential friends.

Each of us has our shadow side. From pre-school

days we are taught to conform, to mould ourselves to other people's specifications, to hide and suppress huge chunks of our true natures. T. S. Eliot put it well in *Burnt Norton*: "Human kind cannot bear much reality". We spend a great deal of time and effort endeavouring to escape reality and pretending to be happy and whole when we are in fact broken and alienated from ourselves.

> The mind is all too often a seething cauldron of unhealed memories of past failure that blight our present equanimity and condemn us to future inadequacy, if not complete impotence. The names of the legion of hosts that possess the unquiet mind are anxiety, fear, envy, resentment, anger, lust, pride, suspicion and ill-will. We have inherited them as part of the conditioning we underwent during the formative years of our upbringing, and their number is steadily increased by the sordid life we live and our unsatisfactory relationships with other people.[2]

Relationships with Others

> So many of us flee from people crying out in pain, people who are broken.
> We hide in a world of distraction and pleasure or in "things to do".[3]

Since we find it so hard to accept ourselves, it is not surprising that we find it equally, if not more, difficult to relate to others. Fear that others may penetrate

25

our mask, expose our shadow side and reject us as worthless, prevents us from seeking a deep and honest relationship with most of those around us. The irony is that we are only too ready ourselves to brand others as unacceptable. We want everyone to be like us and we feel threatened if people adopt different attitudes and standards to our own because they raise questions about the correctness and worth of our own lives, questions we would rather avoid. So we are caught in a vicious circle, we are broken by our own and other people's inability to accept us as we are and yet we contribute to the brokenness of others by refusing to accept them as they are. We try to conform ourselves to the standards of our society and our God and we expect others to follow suit.

This attitude pervades all our relationships to some degree, from the most casual to the most intimate. It is often most vividly illustrated in what should be the most intimate and honest of all relationships – marriage. Very often one marriage partner, albeit unconsciously, will sacrifice their own personality and independent thought and assume that of their partner. Their own taste, interests, friends and opinions become their shadow side. The dominant partner may be flattered by such behaviour and often takes it as an essential expression of love. If the weaker partner's mask should ever slip, or if anger or resentment should lead them to tear the mask off once and for all, the dominant partner will feel threatened, confused, even betrayed. This state of things can hardly be labelled a relationship. The partners are not relating to each other. The dominant partner is simply relating to a mirror image of themselves and the weaker partner has allowed him or herself to be swallowed up by their partner.

Parents often behave in much the same way towards their children. They bring their children up in the (again mostly unconscious) expectation and hope that their offspring will be clones or more successful versions of themselves. If the child dares to question the received attitudes and standards the parents will become defensive and possibly dictatorial. If children should dare to choose a life style very different from that of their parents or one that their parents will not approve of, the parents will often declare themselves to be "failures". They think they have failed as parents because they have produced individual, independent persons and not mere carbon copies of themselves. Sometimes they are so broken by this supposed failure that they blame their children for deliberately hurting them and would rather cut themselves off from their children and pretend that they do not exist than face up to the truth and the challenge of their children's chosen path and accept them as they are.

Whether we acknowledge it or not we long to be loved as we really are, "warts and all", and we also long to love another completely – shadow side and all. Some people are lucky enough to find this perfect (and I use the word in the same sense as the Greek term *telos* meaning "being complete", "whole") relationship quite early on in their lives. It may be a relationship that leads to lifelong commitment in a sexual partnership, it may be a non-sexual relation-

ship. Some think they have found the perfect relationship because it mirrors society's model and so cannot
work out why deep down they feel uneasy or frustrated with the relationship. Others think they have
found the perfect partnership only to realize later that
their relationship is not complete, that those involved
cannot accept each other as they truly are. And others
have to endure the pain and disappointment of a
fruitless search, in which a great many hearts get
broken. It is a risky business offering your whole self
– shadow side included – to another person; you risk
rejection and humiliation. As Hilary observed, "if you
are going to love you are going to get hurt and
broken". Repeated or unexpected rejection can leave
a person so hurt and broken that they can never risk
loving again. They retreat into themselves, into pain
and loneliness.

Loneliness is something we all go through sometimes. It is a symptom of our brokenness. Some people
never manage to escape its clutches. Loneliness is not
to be equated with solitude. There are those who have
learnt to love themselves and others as they are and
can be perfectly content with their own company for
most of the time whilst always being ready to welcome
and relate to others. Others can be surrounded by
family and friends and yet feel bitterly alone because
even though they know and like many people, there
is no one to whom they can really relate, least of all
themselves, in whose company they can feel relaxed
enough to let their mask slip and whom they can
invite into the deepest part of their personality.

As if things were not painful enough, all our

relationships, however perfect, are finite like our-selves. We just do not know what is round the corner, we are not in control of our lives. Forces beyond our control are liable to enter into our lives and into our relationships and break them and us. And we are left mourning what was and what might have been.

As I have already said, social gatherings are often occasions which reveal how little we relate to one another and how preoccupied we are with ourselves. A couple of years ago I was invited to a dinner party to celebrate the fact that a fellow lecturer had been given a permanent contract of employment (these were like gold dust in the institution for which we worked). Although I refused to acknowledge it at the time I resented the fact that my colleague had been given a contract when I had not. I was also worn down by acute pain that had blighted my legs and my life for several months (it later turned out that I had been walking around with a fractured pelvis) and did not feel like partying. But I felt I had to go in case my absence gave the impression that I was jealous. So I assumed a hastily constructed jolly mask and went accompanied by Tom, a friend who at that time was going through a severe emotional crisis and who, like me, would have rather stayed at home and tried to come to terms with his misery and pain. There were a number of people at the party whom I had not met before and I made what I thought to be valiant efforts to be sociable. Yet every time either I or Tom made an attempt to steer the conversation away from the usual conversational ball games, "What do you do?", "Where do you live?", "How many children do you have?'', on to something a little more deep we were listened to politely but someone then made a light-hearted quip and it was back up to the surface and the ball game. It was as if everybody was so frightened of letting their mask slip even slightly that they would not even dare to embark on the usual dinner party subjects. I suppose that what I really wanted was for someone to notice that I was in pain and offer sympathy and support but my walking stick and limp were studiously ignored. I became increasingly irritated and resentful and eventually withdrew from the conversation and took a certain delight in the uncomfortable atmosphere this created and which everyone else pretended not to notice. I found myself so alienated from the people around me that I was in conflict with them. They ceased to be persons with individual needs and concerns which I had a duty to respect and became "insensitive", "irritating" and "stupid" cardboard cut-outs that I could dismiss with a word.

I then realized that Tom too had withdrawn from the conversation, having found the general preoccupation with family life too painful to bear. The climax of the evening came for me when someone went round the room asking each in turn about their hobbies. When it came to Tom's turn he hesitated and I suddenly realized (Tom later confirmed my suspicion) that he was toying with the idea of making an obscene comment, but he managed to check himself and replied "walking"! Even now I amuse myself by wondering how the room would have reacted had he not resisted temptation. I suspect a shocked silence would have been followed by nervous giggles and then the next person would have been quizzed. That night I began to appreciate the French philosopher Jean-Paul Sartre's insistence that "Hell is other people" (*Huis Clos*), people thrown together who cannot relate to one another.

I said I felt myself to be in conflict with my fellow dinner guests who refused to allow the possibility of relationships being formed. Brokenness and alienation lead to conflict – conflict in ourselves as we try to tame and banish our shadow side, conflict with others who refuse to recognize our needs and whose needs we do not acknowledge. Such conflict springing from the depth of our being poisons our lives. It expresses itself in anger, sometimes in violence. Most people acknowledge that we live in a violent society. Our society is violent because it is alienated. Different sections of society treat each other as faceless members of a species that can be described by a series of labels. We do not listen to each other, we do not want to know and respect each other, so misunderstanding and anger result. And yet we want to be listened to and known ourselves. We want to be treated as persons.

Our Broken Bodies

Like the rest of us our bodies are unwhole and unsound. They are liable to break down. The medical professions are at the moment rediscovering the realization of our ancestors that there is a close relation-

31

ship between the inner person and the health of the body. Each affects the other. So a discontented, depressed or distressed person is particularly prone to physical illness, whilst chronic or acute physical discomfort will inevitably cause the sufferer psychological distress. The one manifests the brokenness of the other.

The prospect of illness usually fills a healthy person with dread and many people go to enormous lengths to keep sickness at bay. This dread arises not only because we fear the pain that usually accompanies illness but also because in today's society health is an important aspect of success. To be ill is to be a failure, particularly if it forces one to give up earning a living and to become dependent on the state. We also fear sickness because of the loss of control over our lives that serious illness brings. Chronic pain and disease gradually suck away a person's energy, leaving them unable to do things for themselves and having to rely on others to perform tasks of an intimate, private nature.

Dependence diminishes a person's dignity in their own eyes and often in the eyes of others. Proud men and women in full control of their lives, used to comfort and respect in the familiar and private surroundings of their own home, can suddenly find themselves reduced to frustrated, suffering people who must assume the role of "patient". Often they will find themselves dependent upon others, perhaps on strangers and perhaps moved from their own homes and hospitalized (which means being under the control of strangers, in a strange environment with very little privacy). These strangers may not treat the patient as a person with a right to be respected, informed and consulted but as a body, a lump of flesh that has to be exposed, examined and treated. As Dr Sheila Cassidy has noted,

> Nearly all patients who come to hospital clinics experience a degree of anxiety. They are worried about being unwell, anxious about what will be found and concerned that they will irritate the doctor who is so clever and busy. They fear too that they will look a fool because they cannot explain themselves clearly. In most clinics, however, instead of helping people to feel at ease, we divest them of their carefully chosen clothes, thereby reducing their sense of being a "proper person". Then, when we have rendered them even more vulnerable, we expect them to discuss their intimate problems and expose their bodies in the presence of strangers. And if then they exhibit their anxiety we write them off as being neurotic![4]

Acute pain takes total control of the sufferer, turning him in upon himself. Thus pain cuts the patient off from those around him and makes him very difficult to reach. It affects the whole person and dominates the whole person – as one car crash victim put it,

> If anybody had asked me my name then, I would have said, "My name is pain". I was nothing but pain – a throbbing being. Nobody can ever know what it is like.[5]

Serious or chronic illness cruelly strips away the masks we have built up. The only mask that it is possible to assume is that of the "good patient" who never causes any "trouble" and who keeps his fears, doubts and complaints to himself.

The most painful aspect of serious illness is that it inevitably brings people face to face with their mortality. Death becomes a real possibility, not simply a dot on the horizon that can be easily ignored. The fear of self-annihilation that most of us manage to suppress most of the time surfaces with merciless force, casting a dark question mark over the meaning of existence. This is why relationships between patients and their family and friends often become difficult and strained. A sick person will often become frustrated and impatient with carers and visitors who studiously avoid the subject of illness and try to "cheer up" the patient with trivia. The patient desperately needs to discuss urgent and ultimate questions: their chances of recovery; the possibility of death and what that involves; their hopes, fears and expectations. They may long to reach into the depths of the people they love, having been made painfully aware by the prospect of death of the superficiality of most relationships. But the carer may not be ready to face these questions themselves and so tries to distract the patient from this line of thought. For a similar reason, people are often reluctant to visit a sick person. They are afraid of coming face to face with someone wrestling with the ultimate questions of existence because they are afraid of having to face these questions in their own lives. A sick person therefore has to cope with apparent rejection by friends when they are most in need of them.

Sickness therefore can bring with it fear, frustration, rejection, humiliation, loneliness, separation from the familiar and beloved. Above all it brings a need to get down to what matters, to make every word and moment count.

The word "pain" derives from the Latin word *"poena"* meaning punishment. The idea that illness is sent by God as a punishment for sin is rooted in the Old Testament and is a theme that runs throughout the book of Psalms:

> O Lord, rebuke me not in thy anger,
> nor chasten me in thy wrath! . . .
> There is no soundness in my flesh
> because of thy indignation;
> there is no health in my bones
> because of my sin . . .
> My wounds grow foul and fester
> because of my foolishness, . . .
> My friends and companions stand
> aloof from my plague,
> and my kinsmen stand afar off.
>
> Psalm 38:1, 3, 5 and 11

The fact that serious sickness branded a person a sinner meant that they were shunned by the ancient Israelite community and some were excluded from the ritual of worship. So a sick person was cut off from both God and humanity.

The Old Testament also contains a slightly different interpretation of the meaning of illness. In the book of Job, we are told that God tests Job's loyalty to him by allowing Satan to afflict this blameless and upright Israelite with the most awful troubles, including a terrible skin disease that makes his life unbearable. Despite all this provocation Job steadfastly refused to curse God even though his neighbours tried to convince him that he was being punished for sin; he is eventually rewarded for his faithfulness by having his fortune doubled. The great philosophers Plato and Aristotle also regarded pain and suffering as a form of testing and chastening.

Despite advances in medical knowledge a surprising number of religious people, including some Christians, still think in these terms with regard to illness. The Order of the Visitation of the Sick in the Book of Common Prayer instructs the minister to address the sick person with these words.

> Wherefore, whatsoever your sickness is, know you certainly, that it is God's visitation . . . know you certainly, that if you truly repent you of your sins, and bear your sickness patiently, trusting in God's mercy . . . it shall turn to your profit, and help you forward in the right way that leadeth unto everlasting life . . . whom the Lord loveth he chasteneth, and scourgeth every son whom he receiveth.

Whether Christians are ever justified in taking this attitude to illness is a question which will be tackled in the next chapter. For now it is enough to observe that a sick person who believes her affliction has been sent by God, for whatever reason, bears an enormous burden. Belief that one's physical condition is punishment for sin will heighten the feeling of failure that every ill person experiences and might possibly lead to a terrible sense of despair – if God is against you, what hope have you got? A terrible sense of guilt is also inevitable. If, on the other hand, you believe that God is testing your faith through illness, then you will be under an enormous pressure to "keep cheerful", "bear up", "be strong" and to fight all the negative feelings that are the normal accompaniment to illness. In other words, yet another mask is assumed, designed to fool, to fool oneself, others and God.

None of us knows what will happen after our bodies die. We can guess, imagine and hope, but we cannot know. The objective evidence suggests that the self is annihilated and the body decomposes. Where once there was a person who laughed, cried, loved and lost, there is nothing except slowly rotting flesh. Because human beings have the unique ability to know they exist there is nothing they fear more than the loss of existence, of falling into nothingness. It is from this base fear that all other fears stem: the fear of rejection, of failure, of losing independence and control, are all fears of being reduced, of sliding closer to non-existence. Throughout our lives we suffer many little deaths like these – failing an exam, losing a job, losing friends and relations by death or other means, losing health, strength and independence. And then comes the final and apparently everlasting death when human beings are utterly destroyed, broken beyond repair and dissolved into non-existence.

The Relationship with God

For many people in today's western world their relationship with God is not a problem. God has no meaning for such people. Either they do not believe in the existence of such a being or else admit to believing that "there is something" but are not prepared to commit themselves as to what and they certainly do not have any relationship with it. A Christian, of course, cannot accept either of these positions. The theologian Paul Tillich defined God as that which is our ultimate concern. Whether we are theists or not, we all have some concern that dominates all others, that matters more to us than anything else – this is our god. Christians have made the God revealed by Jesus Christ their ultimate concern and maintain that all other ultimate concerns are idols, that whereas the God revealed by Christ offers broken humanity healing and freedom from fear, all other gods or ultimate concerns enslave their devotees and increase their brokenness.

I think of John. John does not believe in the Christian God or, he would claim, in any other god. All his time and energy is devoted to making money. His job is to make money for a multinational firm. It takes him all over the world. He starts work at dawn and does not finish until late at night. In the dog-eat-dog world of high finance he is reluctant to establish friendships with his colleagues. His firm requires him to assume a mask, the mask of a dynamic young salesman who believes totally in his product. Hair has to be dyed, weight lost, clothes carefully chosen. The product has to be "plugged" at every opportunity. Radios, glasses, jackets, caps, mugs all adorned with the firm's logo grace his home. John judges everything and everyone by their financial value. His wife and children are regarded as assets and well-chosen products. His love for them is expressed through money, his wife is given a beautiful house and furniture, his children are sent to expensive schools. Things that are free, like the joys of family life, art, nature, literature, friendship are considered worthless, as are people who earn little money, no matter what their occupation. John does not realize it but he worships money. Money is his god, his ultimate concern. Money has enslaved him and rules his life, preventing him from being a complete person and treating others as persons. He lives in constant fear of losing his job and his money because this would mean becoming worthless in his eyes. Anything can become an idol: work, drink, drugs, another person, a fear, a dream, oneself, the Christian God wrongly understood.

Christians commit themselves to a personal God who holds the world in his hands, who is the ground of all existence, who does not enslave but liberates, who heals their brokenness and whose unconditional love of everyone makes all equally important. But a Christian's relationship with God is just as stormy and precarious as any human relationship. It is just as hard to remove your mask and open up to God as it is to those around you and the fear of rejection is more intense because it is an infinite, eternal, ultimate rejection. I will argue later that this fear is groundless.

It arises mainly because, I feel, we read too much of ourselves into God.

The image of God as judge has been a popular one in the history of Christianity. One of the most memorable images used by Jesus is to be found in Matthew 25 where the King judges men and women according to their treatment of one another. Some are taken into his kingdom, others are banished into the "eternal fire". A judge decides whether one is acceptable or not. A judge is therefore to be feared and placated. Any relationship based upon fear is a distorted, broken, imperfect relationship because one is afraid to be oneself, to speak one's mind. One tries to conform to the expectations of the judge. Many Christians think of God as above all else a judge. These Christians are involved in a broken relationship with God.

Even Christians who play down the image of God as judge and who prefer to think of God as Jesus did, as father, do not necessarily achieve a perfect relationship with him. It is true that, generally speaking, a father is a much more approachable figure than a judge. You can be much more relaxed in the company of a father. (Although it is important to emphasize that this is not universally true. For some their fathers are figures of fear, hate and hurt.) Fathers are more likely to forgive their errant offspring than a judge is to let off an offender. A father will want what is best for the child. However, think for a moment about your relationship with your own father. No matter how normal it was it is unlikely to have been a completely open relationship in which no

40

masks were assumed. I think of my own father, who is the most gentle and forgiving of men but there are whole areas of myself, my life and thought that I keep from him out of fear of hurting or distressing him and because I know he would not understand them. (And he too keeps large areas of himself hidden from me.) Many people's relationships with their fathers break down, sometimes irreparably, either in infancy or later on in life. A parent-child relationship is not perfect. Parents may love their child deeply and yet still assume the role of critic and judge. Human experience of fatherhood, or indeed motherhood, is not of a complete, perfect, unbroken relationship. Therefore when we approach God as father we assume the same sort of masks as we do before our own parents, although we may not recognize what we are doing. As a result we are not ourselves before God and alienate ourselves from him.

Just as we feel betrayed and rejected by friends and relations when they fail to meet our needs, just as we are only too ready to blame others for our own misfortune, so we feel abandoned by God whenever disaster strikes. How can a supposedly loving God apparently sit back and watch as his creatures suffer so badly? The apparent betrayal by God is the hardest to understand and the most difficult to forgive.

Many people are prevented from entering into a relationship with God by the behaviour of those who claim to be close to him. The Church is not an attractive institution; it often appears self-satisfied, navel-picking, wealthy and powerful, misogynistic and judgemental. Who would really want to know a God who attracts followers like that?

So we must accept that our relationship with God is just as prone to brokenness as is our relationship with ourselves, our body and with others. Before the one who knows all, and from whom nothing can be hid, it is natural, like Adam and Eve, to be afraid, to hide, to pretend he does not exist or to turn him into something more comfortable, to make him assume a role or mask – a judge or father whom one can hide from behind the masks of personality.

The sketch I have drawn of the human condition is pretty black. It would be easy to agree with Sartre that humankind is nothing but a "useless passion" (*L'Être et le néant*), lonely and broken, hiding from itself, others and God, and destined for nothingness. The fact is that when we dare to take a close and honest look at existence we realize that it can be very bleak. No wonder we prefer to run away from it into the world of masks and superficiality. Think about what happens when we hear about a terrible disaster, a crash or an earthquake. For a time we are shocked and appalled as the fragility and brokenness of human life is brought home to us with an intensity which cannot be ignored. But then we can bear it no longer, we banish the awful spectacle from our minds, we busy ourselves in our daily routine, we try not to think about it. We cannot bear much reality. Yes, it is all pretty depressing, or rather it would be if one person had not shown us what reality is all about. That person is Jesus Christ.

2

Jesus Christ: The Healer
of Brokenness

The Lord builds up Jerusalem;
he gathers the outcasts of Israel.
He heals the brokenhearted,
and binds up their wounds . . .
The Lord lifts up the downtrodden,
he casts the wicked to the ground.

Psalm 147:2–3 and 6

For God so loved the world that he gave his only
Son, that whoever believes in him should not
perish but have eternal life. For God sent the Son
into the world, not to condemn the world, but
that the world might be saved through him.

John 3:16–17

Christians cannot share Sartre's pessimistic diagnosis
of the human condition because of the nature of the
God in whom they believe. Christians profess belief
in the God who first revealed himself to the ancient
Hebrews, the creator and sustainer of all that exists,
who cares deeply for his creation. Even though
humankind has become alienated from God he wishes
to *save* it and reconcile it to himself.

43

The Bible contains two distinct but related concepts
of salvation. Sometimes salvation is understood as
deliverance, release and preservation. God is understood as the God of the Exodus, delivering his people
from the things that threaten them and undermine
their relationship with him – the enemy, battle,
famine, sickness, captivity or, in the New Testament,
sin. At other times, salvation is to be understood as
wholeness, soundness and good health. (Indeed, this
is the meaning of the Latin word *salus* from which
our English word "salvation" is derived.) These two
understandings of salvation are of course closely
related. In this chapter I want to explore the concept
of God as the one who heals and delivers.

Christians proclaim that God saves humankind by
reaching down into the depths of human brokenness
and healing it. God does this not by denying the worth
of the human condition, not by providing human
beings with a means of escaping it, but by making it
his own condition.

God became human in Jesus of Nazareth. This is
the heart of the Christian faith. Through Jesus, God
revealed to the world what sort of God he is. He is a
God who is not "above" the world, supervising and
intervening when necessary or requested yet unaffec-
ted by what happens in it. On the contrary, he is a
God who is as involved in the world and the human
condition as we are. He is a God who knows and
understands what it is to be human, for he has been
human himself.

God was truly human. This is the paradox at the

base of Christian belief. God became human and therefore experienced all the pain, alienation and brokenness that being human involves. The first three Gospels show us through the stories of the temptations (Matthew 4:1–11) that Jesus, like us, struggled with the desire to assume masks that would hide his vulnerability and weakness – his true nature. He, like us, was a member of a family, a society, a religion and a culture that fashioned and moulded his character and opinions. Like us, Jesus found himself alienated from some of his fellow human beings – represented in the Gospels by scribes, Sadducees, Pharisees and, to some extent, the Gentiles. He cannot relate to these people and finds himself in conflict with them. He certainly seems to have resorted to stereotyping.

> But woe to you Pharisees! for you tithe mint and rue and every herb, and neglect justice and the love of God; these you ought to have done, without neglecting the others. Woe to you Pharisees! for you love the best seat in the synagogues and salutations in the market places. Woe to you! for you are like graves which are not seen, and men walk over them without knowing it. Luke 11:42–4

> And in praying do not heap up empty phrases as the Gentiles do; for they think that they will be heard for their many words. . . . These twelve Jesus sent out, charging them, "Go nowhere among the Gentiles, and enter no town of the Samaritans, but go rather to the lost sheep of the house of Israel." Matthew 6:7 and 10:5–6

45

Jesus knew the pain and despair of losing loved ones through death (John 11:33–6). He knew the disappointment, hurt and frustration of being misunderstood not only by strangers but also by his family and friends for whom he became an embarrassment (John 7:5). He knew what it was like to be dismissed simply because of the part of the country he came from and the social status of his family (John 1:46 and Mark 6:2–4).

After being welcomed and treated as a hero, Jesus experienced rejection by society, by the authorities of his religion, by his family and friends. He knew what it was like to be mocked, hated and taunted. Jesus was not immune from the fear of death and annihilation. We are told that while waiting for his inevitable arrest Jesus was "greatly distressed and troubled" (Mark 14:33), so much so that "his sweat became like great drops of blood falling down upon the ground" (Luke 22:44) and he prayed desperately to be rescued from what was to come. At the time the Jews had no concept of an immortal soul continuing to exist after one's body died. For the Jews, human beings were a complete unity, when one died one was annihilated. The Pharisees believed that God would raise the righteous but that was a gratuitous act on the part of God and no one could assume that they were going to be raised.

Jesus knew all about failure. He died the death of a failure. Only political subversives and common criminals were executed by crucifixion. The kingdom of God which he was so sure was about to be established did not arrive. (So sure was Jesus that the kingdom was coming that, when sending his disciples out to teach, preach and heal, he promised them "you will not have gone through all the towns of Israel, before the Son of Man comes" (Matthew 10:23).)

Jesus' body was tortured, suffered agonizing pain and was finally destroyed. He knew what it is like to die slowly and painfully, to die an ugly, lonely yet public death. He knew what it was to feel your body breaking apart and your mind splintering. He, like all human beings, stood over the abyss of non-existence. He lay in the tomb for three days. It was a common belief at that time that some form of life remained in the corpse for the first three days after death. All life had gone from Jesus.

Jesus' relationship with God also experienced brokenness. He wanted his God to intervene, to establish his kingdom and to vindicate him and rescue him from failure, rejection, suffering and death. When Jesus' prayers went unanswered he felt rejected and forsaken by his father in heaven. At the moment of his death he felt utterly alienated from God. According to Mark, the first of the Gospels to be written, the last words Jesus spoke were a terrible proclamation of doubt, fear and alienation which encapsulate the human experience:

> And at the ninth hour Jesus cried with a loud voice, "Elo-i, Elo-i, lama sabachthani?" which means, "My God, my God, why hast thou forsaken me?" Mark 15:34

Which was followed by a wordless cry of despair and agony (Mark 15:37).

47

Let's just stop and think for a moment about the implications of all this. God in Jesus Christ became a human being. He was truly human; not merely clothed in humanity but totally human. He experienced all the emotions, desire, pains, doubts, confusion that we experience. This included alienation from others and from God – from himself. What an odd and illogical thing to assert! How can God who is perfectly whole experience alienation from himself? I don't know either. I cannot get my mind around this paradox but nor can I understand how God became fully human. Yet if we are going to assert with the Nicene Creed that the "true God" "was made man", and was not merely pretending to be human like so many of the gods of mythology, then we have to accept that God experienced all the pain and alienation of being human and that includes being alienated from God. Once you start qualifying the statement "God was truly human" with "in all things but . . ." you make nonsense of the doctrine of the incarnation and erode the basis of the Christian faith.

Another startling implication of the belief that God became human in Christ is that God actually suffered and died. Why have centuries of Christians found this implication impossible to accept? Quite early on in its history, in the third century AD, the Christian Church came under the influence of the Greek philosophy known as Neo-Platonism. Neo-Platonists taught that the Absolute (whom Christians equated with God) was utterly transcendent, virtually unknowable, eternal, unchangeable, impassible (that is, incapable of suffering), omnipotent, omniscient, perfect and self-sufficient, totally "other" than the world and humankind. The Absolute had brought the world into being through his Logos or Word (which Christians identified with Christ). This concept of God, which was taken on board by Christianity and became the Christian concept of God, is very hard to align with the involved, loving God revealed by Jesus. The early Christian theologians found it hard enough to explain the incarnation in Neo-Platonic terms but they came positively unstuck when they had to explain the suffering and death of Christ in these terms. They held that the Logos of God had become incarnate in Jesus Christ but, believing that God was impassible they could not assert that the Logos had suffered and died. Some argued that the Logos entered Jesus at his baptism and departed before his crucifixion. Others argued that Christ had two natures, human and divine, and the latter did not suffer and die as the former did. Eventually the Church declared at the Council of Chalcedon in 451 that Christ was one person in two natures, divine and human, which were united "unconfusedly, unchangeably, indivisibly, inseparably" but still considered it heretical to assert that God had suffered on the cross and died. The remoulding of the Christian faith in Neo-Platonic terms meant that it was no longer possible for the Christian Church to preach a thoroughgoing doctrine of the incarnation such as is found in St Paul's simple proclamation, "in Christ God was reconciling the world to himself" (2 Corinthians 5:19).

So we must conclude that if Christ reveals what

God is like, God knows what it is to suffer, to be alienated from himself and his fellow human beings, and God knows what it is to die. Indeed, we *must* conclude this because if God knows nothing of humanity, brokenness, suffering, alienation and death then he cannot have conquered and healed human brokenness. In the words of the early Church Father, Gregory of Nazianzus, what is not assumed is not healed.

> Christ's own being on the Cross contained all the clashing contrarities and scandalous fates of human existence. Life Himself was identified with death; the Light of the world was enveloped in darkness. The feet of the Man who said "I am the Way" feared to tread upon it and prayed, "If it be possible, not that way". The Water of Life was thirsty. The Bread of Life was hungry. The divine Lawgiver was Himself unjustly outlawed. The Holy One was identified with the unholy . . . So much meaningless suffering, senseless injustice, unmerited pain, and pointless deprivation, has, by this Cross, conferred upon it the possibility of transformation into deeper unities of meaning, good sense, relief of pain, and victorious acceptance.[1]

As the twentieth-century theologian Jürgen Moltmann has noted, the god of the Platonist and the Christian Platonist is of no use to humankind because he knows nothing about what it is to be human. Life becomes a useless passion because God is not involved in it and is utterly alienated from it.

A God who cannot choose to suffer and die is inferior to a man if man grasps this suffering and death as his own possibilities and chooses them himself . . . a God who is only omnipotent is in himself an incomplete being, for he cannot experience helplessness and powerlessness.[2]

The God revealed by Christ is in fact paradoxically much more powerful and much more glorious than the god of the Platonists because he can choose to empty himself of his divinity and become one with humanity.

> God is not more glorious than he is in this self-surrender.
> God is not more powerful than he is in this help-lessness.
> God is not more divine than he is in this humanity.[3]

One of the earliest "all but . . ." qualifications to the assertion that in Christ God became human appears in the epistles of the New Testament: "[Jesus] has been tempted as we are, yet without sin" (Hebrews 4:15); "[Christ] committed no sin; no guile was found on his lips" (1 Peter 2:22); "For our sake he made him to be sin who knew no sin" (2 Corinthians 5:21). As far as we know Jesus never declared himself to be sinless. However soon after his death the followers of Jesus came to understand him in terms of the Suffering Servant. This is the mysterious figure described in Isaiah 42, 49, 50 and 53 who is chosen by God to be "wounded for our transgressions" and "bruised for our iniquities" (Isaiah 53:5). An innocent man, "he had done no violence and there was no deceit in his mouth" (Isaiah 53:9), who, like a sacrificial lamb or the scapegoat on the Day of Atonement, bears the sins of all the people of Israel and takes the punishment that they all deserve. After the servant's death God rewards him for his work. The servant as a sacrificial offering had to be sinless otherwise he would simply be enduring the punishment due for his own sin. So Jesus came to be understood as the Suffering Servant who had borne the sins of the world and he too came to be understood as sinless. Also, once the early Christians came to perceive that Christ had revealed God in his own person, it seemed obvious that God himself could not be involved in sin.

I said earlier that these "all buts" undermine the reality of the incarnation, and the statement that "in Christ God was like us in all things but sin" is no exception. St Paul noted that all men, "both Jews and Greeks, are under the power of sin" (Romans 3:9). Sin is an intrinsic part of the human condition. So to say that one man existed who was without sin is tantamount to saying that this man was not truly and fully human.

What exactly do we mean by "sin"? In the Old Testament sin is understood as disobedience of God's Law which was given to Moses and elaborated upon by the prophets. Sin put one in a wrong relationship with God and the community which was founded upon his Law. By Jesus' day an oral Law had been developed to complement the written Law and to apply it in everyday situations. We know that Jesus

broke this oral Law by healing on the Sabbath, mixing
with the unclean and refusing to fast. So the Pharisees
who cherished this code of laws would certainly have
regarded Jesus as a sinner. St Paul understood sin as
a power which has dominion over humanity. The
only thing people should allow to have dominion over
them, should allow to become their "ultimate concern", is Christ, anything else is an idol. Christ had
none of the usual idols – money, health, prestige,
another person, a dream – but he did share with all
humanity the one idol that it is virtually impossible
to escape: the self. Concern and obsession with oneself
will always be in danger of clouding humanity's perception of and relation to God, it is an occupational
hazard of being human. Christ was fully human and
therefore he cannot have avoided, at least occasion-
ally, falling into self-centredness and therefore falling
into sin. There are times when Jesus seems to be so
preoccupied with his own ministry that he treats his
family and friends with remarkable insensitivity.
When his mother and brothers try and talk to him he
dismisses them with the words "Who are my mother
and my brothers?" And looking around on those who
sat about him, he said, "Here are my mother and my
brothers! Whoever does the will of God is my brother,
and sister, and mother" (Mark 3:33–5). And when he
heard that his close friend Lazarus was ill and that
Lazarus' sisters Mary and Martha had sent for him,
Jesus did not set out immediately to them, "when he
heard that he was ill, he stayed two days longer in
the place where he was" (John 11:6). In the days and
hours leading up to Jesus' death he becomes, quite

naturally, obsessed with himself, his life and his impending death.

Another way to look at sin is as alienation from God which causes the one who is alienated to act in what we would define as "sinful" ways. As we have seen there were certainly times in his life when Christ was alienated from God and therefore was undoubtedly involved in human sinfulness. In classical Greek the verb *hamartano*, "to sin", is often used to mean "to miss the mark", in the sense of failing to attain one's goal or fulfil one's potential. Even if we adopt this definition of sin we cannot exclude Jesus Christ from it. All human beings fail to fulfil their potential in some, if not all, areas of their life. Brokenness and finitude prevent such complete fulfilment. Jesus was both broken and finite.

Jesus was as involved in sin as the rest of humanity. To say otherwise is to deny that he was truly human. A student once complained to me, "We are supposed to follow and be like Christ but he had an unfair advantage over us because he didn't have to walk against the wind of sin." It may seem a nonsense, it may seem blasphemous, it is a paradox but I am certain that it is true: the God revealed by Christ knows what it is to "walk against the wind of sin".

God in Jesus Christ is completely destroyed by being human, broken apparently beyond repair. But this is not the end of the story. For the God who dies in misery, broken by pain, raises himself from brokenness and non-existence to new life and wholeness.

In order to appreciate what it meant to the friends and followers of Jesus when they realized that Jesus had been raised from the dead it is important to remember that the Jews, unlike the Greeks, made no distinction between the mortal body and the immortal soul. A human being was one and thus when death came it was considered to be final and total. So when God raised Jesus from the dead he was not simply reuniting Jesus' body with his already immortal soul. In raising Jesus God was offering him and through him all humanity the possibility of a new existence; a healed, whole, unalienated existence. All idols are conquered, even the last idol, the self. So different is this new healed existence from our broken existence that, at first, even his closest friends do not recognize the risen Christ (Luke 24:13–32 and John 20:15–18). The risen Christ acknowledges no barriers between people and no barriers between God and his creation. This is symbolically expressed in the resurrection stories by the fact that locked doors fail to keep Christ from his disciples (John 20:19).

Through the resurrection of Jesus, God reveals that he is the one who brings life from death and wholeness from brokenness. The important fact so often overlooked in this revelation is that wholeness, healing and salvation only come after and through the human experience of alienation, suffering and death. One cannot be completely healed until one has been utterly broken. Jesus is healed but we are told that even in his resurrected state he still bore the scars of his crucifixion, the scars of his humanity (John 20:27).

Jesus' earthly ministry was devoted to healing, to offering to those around him a glimpse of the healing and wholeness that will be made complete in the resurrection. If we look carefully at the healing narratives in the Gospels we can observe that Jesus' healing usually took place on two levels, internal and external, the body is healed but usually only after the personality has been made whole. A perfect example of Jesus' approach is to be found in the story of the healing of the paralytic:

> And they came, bringing to him a paralytic carried by four men. And when they could not get near him because of the crowd, they removed the roof above him; and when they had made an opening, they let down the pallet on which the paralytic lay. And when Jesus saw their faith, he said to the paralytic, "My son, your sins are forgiven." Now some of the scribes were sitting there, questioning in their hearts, "Why does this man speak thus? It is blasphemy! Who can forgive sins but God alone?" And immediately Jesus, perceiving in his spirit that they thus questioned within themselves, said to them, "Why do you question thus in your hearts? Which is easier, to say to the paralytic, 'Your sins are forgiven,' or to say, 'Rise, take up your pallet and walk'? But that you may know that the Son of man has authority on earth to forgive sins" – he said to the paralytic – "I say to you, rise, take up your pallet and go home." And he rose, and immediately took up the pallet and went out before them

all; so that they were all amazed and glorified God, saying, "We never saw anything like this!"

Mark 2:3–12

When Jesus first sees the man on the pallet being lowered towards him he does not immediately focus upon the man's disability. He looks beyond the disability into the depths of the man's being, he sees that man as he really is. In order to appreciate how extraordinary Jesus' behaviour is, imagine yourself in a similar situation. Into the room in which you are sitting now a couple of people wheel a severely disabled person on a trolley cum wheelchair. This person's body is twisted and deformed. The face stares upwards, the mouth is twisted, the eyes rolling. These would be the things that you and I would notice straight away. At once we would label this person "severely disabled" or "handicapped" or "crippled". We would probably assume that the person would know nothing of what was going on around them. We might feel sorry for those who had to look after "the patient". We might be slightly disgusted by the figure and we might possibly entertain the thought that it would have been better for everyone if this person had died at birth. In short, our reaction would be to treat the person on the trolley as a mistake, an accident, a blemish on the human species that should not be there. Because we cannot face up to the fragility and brokenness of humanity and more particularly of ourselves, we treat this person, not as a person at all, but as a rotting vegetable, as something that has nothing to do with us, never mind equality with us.

57

Many years ago I found myself in a church in Liverpool sitting next to a grieving family who had recently lost their newborn baby through cot death. Their eldest child was physically disabled and confined to a wheelchair but able in every other respect. When the family left the pew to receive communion the lady sitting next to me leant over and whispered, "Wouldn't you think that God would have taken the cripple and left them the healthy baby?" Many people assume that disabled people are people of no worth and are therefore unacceptable and should be kept apart from "normal" people. No doubt this was the attitude of the people who, Mark tells us, gathered at Jesus' home to hear him preach, and they pushed the paralytic out of the way so that they could get a good seat, "After all, he probably can't hear or see, so what's the point of him coming here anyway and getting in the way?"

If we are honest we will acknowledge that there is at least a trace of this attitude in all of us, however enlightened we might profess to be. We would certainly have labelled this person as "disabled" the moment we saw him. Jesus does none of these things. He is completely unconcerned with the man's physical condition, rather he pronounces that the man's sins are forgiven. Why does he do this and what does he mean? Earlier in this chapter I tried to define exactly what sin is and I concluded that it is simply a manifestation of human brokenness, idolatry and alienation. If we accept this definition of sin we must now ask what Jesus meant by forgiveness? I think the definition of forgiveness given by Jean Vanier beautifully expresses in words the understanding of forgiveness that Jesus expressed in actions:

> Forgiveness is understanding and holding
> the pain of another;
> it is compassion.
> Forgiveness is the acceptance of our brokenness,
> yours and mine.
> Forgiveness is letting go of unrealistic expec-
> tations of others
> and of the desire that they be other than they
> are.
> Forgiveness is liberating others to be themselves,
> not making them feel guilty for what may have
> been . . .
> Forgiveness is peace-making:
> struggling to create unity,
> to build one body,
> to heal the broken body of humanity.[4]

When Jesus told the man on the pallet that his sins were forgiven he was in effect saying this, "It is all right to be you. I love you as you are and God loves you as you are. We understand your weakness and vulnerability. There is no need to be afraid and bury yourself under masks because God and I love all those aspects of yourself that you have made into your shadow side, we love the maskless you utterly and unconditionally. So there is no need to be weighted down by guilt, alienation and despair. Be yourself, live your life honestly, openly and fearlessly because we will never reject you. But if you slip back into the shadows do not worry because we are with you in the

59

darkness and want to bring you back into the light."
Forgiveness is the love and acceptance of people as
they are. Such forgiveness is liberating because it
enables people to have the courage to try to escape
their shadow life of masks and alienation, doubt and
fear – the "inauthentic" existence – and live an "authentic" existence.

The religious authorities could not cope with this.
They could not cope with the idea that God loves
and accepts people as they are. The scribes, priests,
Sadducees and Pharisees wielded immense power
over many people by interpreting and proclaiming
in God's name what was and was not acceptable
behaviour, who was and who was not acceptable to
the Lord. They, of course, were the most acceptable
of all. Now Jesus was daring to proclaim to this paralytic who had obviously sinned pretty seriously for
God to have punished him with his physical state,
who could not keep the Law, who was no more than
a vegetable, that he was as important, as acceptable,
as precious in the eyes of God as those who dedicated
every minute of their lives to the keeping of the Law.
Jesus' forgiveness threatened all they stood for, all
they had grounded their lives upon. Jesus threatened
the validity of their idol, the Law.

Jesus was not unique in having the gift of healing.
As he points out to those around him, he could have
healed the man on the stretcher of his physical condition very easily but the man would still have been
as broken as ever, still trapped in his shadow life.
Jesus was not a cosmetic surgeon. He did not come
to make people look physically "acceptable" to others,

to provide them with a means of escape from their
human condition by healing their superficial wounds.
He was a saviour and he came to bring wholeness
and healing to the whole person, not through escape
but through acceptance and love. The paralytic *is*
physically healed. His inner healing manifests itself
in external healing. But even if Jesus had not healed
his physical paralysis the man would still have been
truly healed of his inner brokenness, his inner "paralysis" that was preventing him living an authentic
existence, healed by the love and acceptance of God,
acceptance that included his physical disability.

> "I say to you, rise, take up your pallet and go
> home". And he rose, and immediately took up
> the pallet and went out before them all."
>
> Mark 2:11–12

The man rises up to new life. He experiences a foretaste of the resurrection that is to come, that God will
achieve in Christ and offer to all.

If we look briefly at a few of Jesus' other physical
healings recorded in the Gospels we shall see that in
these too Jesus heals not just the outer brokenness,
indeed that is a secondary concern, but the inner
brokenness as well.

> And a leper came to him beseeching him, and
> kneeling said to him, "If you will, you can make
> me clean." Moved with pity, he stretched out his
> hand and touched him, and said to him, "I will;
> be clean." And immediately the leprosy left him,
> and he was made clean. Mark 1:40–2

At first sight this might appear to be a straightforward "cosmetic" healing. Jesus does not pronounce forgiveness of the man's sins. But, in fact, this healing is much more than a physical healing. Lepers were the most marginalized people in ancient Israel. They were considered to be unclean and because of the infectious nature of the disease they were banished from towns and villages to live in caves in the wilderness. Anyone who touched a leper was also declared to be unclean and whilst in that state could not take part in the religious cult and was therefore believed to be cut off from God. Lepers had to carry bells to warn people that they were approaching. They were, therefore, the most dehumanized, ostracized and feared people in society. As well as this rejection they had to endure the agony of the disease itself which slowly but systematically ate its way through their bodies leaving them horribly scarred and mutilated.

We are told that Jesus was "moved with pity" when he saw the leper. In some of the ancient manuscripts these words are replaced with the assertion that Jesus was "angry". Why would Jesus be angry at seeing the leper? Quite possibly because it made him suddenly fully aware of man's inhumanity to man, of the treatment of this leper by the society and religion of which he was a member, treatment that was meted out in God's name. Few people would even speak to a leper. Jesus not only speaks to him, he *touches* him, thus making himself unclean and risking the possibility of catching the disease himself. Imagine what that touch must have meant to a man who would not have been touched since the day his leprosy had been

confirmed by a priest and would not have expected
to be touched again. Imagine what it must have
meant to a person used to people running away from
him, staring at him with hostile eyes, perhaps even
taunting and mocking him. That touch said so much.
It said, "God loves you and I love you as you are, as
a leper, as a suffering, broken man. To God you are
not an outcast, you are not unclean, you are not
disgusting, on the contrary you are loved, acceptable
and precious". By that touch Jesus was pronouncing
the same forgiveness he gave to the paralytic and once
again the inner healing and wholeness brought by his
touch manifest themselves in physical healing.

There are two recorded incidents in the Gospels of
Jesus actually raising people from the dead. The first
is found in Luke 7:11–17 which tells of Jesus raising
the only son of a widow from Nain. The second is
recorded in John 11. Here Jesus raises his friend
Lazarus. John makes a point of asserting that Lazarus
had been dead for four days so Lazarus was utterly
and indisputably dead. These two figures are the
greatest symbols the Gospels provide of the new life,
the authentic form of existence and wholeness that
Jesus offers. Even those who are broken beyond
despair, destroyed completely, can be raised to a foretaste of new life and wholeness. Lazarus and the boy
from Nain are *raised from the dead* to continue their
previous, albeit transformed, existence – they are not
resurrected. Christ is resurrected to a new type of life
altogether, a completely whole and healed life. Such
a life is not possible in the present existence.

> And immediately there was in their synagogue a
> man with an unclean spirit; and he cried out,
> "What have you to do with us, Jesus of Nazareth?
> Have you come to destroy us? I know who you
> are, the Holy One of God." But Jesus rebuked
> him, saying, "Be silent, and come out of him!"
> And the unclean spirit, convulsing him and
> crying with a loud voice, came out of him.
>
> Mark 1:23–6

The Gospels tell us that Jesus healed many people by
driving out demons. Today few people in the West
can accept the existence of demons or attribute mental
or physical illness to them as people used to. What
then are we to make of these healings, what significance can they have for us? The ancients believed
that demons took possession of their victims and
eventually destroyed them. People possessed by
demons were shunned and feared by the rest of
society. In chapter one I argued that one of the
reasons why people have broken or non-existent
relationships with God is that they have adopted other
gods, gods that take control of their lives, reducing
the person to the status of a slave and unable to break
free from its destructive power. I would like to offer
one possible interpretation of these stories. I would
suggest that the "demoniacs" of the Gospels were, in
fact, people who had become enslaved by such idols,
people who had simply become obsessed with one
particular thing which had come to dominate their
lives, isolating them from others, destroying their own
personality. I would suggest that the demoniac in the

synagogue at Capernaum was a man who had made the Law his idol. He rightly perceived that Jesus had come to divest the Law of its idolatrous power and this is why he screams out in fear: the meaning in his life is about to be challenged.

In Mark 5 we read of another demoniac Jesus came into contact with, the Gerasene demoniac. This was a man who lived among the tombs, crying out and wounding himself with stones. When asked his name he replied, "My name is Legion; for we are many" (Mark 5:9). I would suggest that this man was obsessed with himself. He hated himself and the many masks he assumed and so he wounded himself and thought of himself not as one man but as many.

Mark 9 tells of a boy possessed by an evil spirit which rendered him deaf and dumb. Perhaps in his early childhood this boy had suffered a terrible trauma that had so affected him psychologically that he had no desire to hear or speak of anything again. He was therefore psychologically imprisoned by this incident, it was controlling and ruining his life. So much did it dominate his life that when Jesus released him from its control the boy became "like a corpse" so most of them said, "He is dead" (Mark 9:26). All meaning seemed to have gone out of his life.

What does Jesus do to release these people from the control of their idols? Quite simply he challenges the worth of their own idols and he challenges them in his own person. Jesus represents authentic existence based upon love, honesty and acceptance emanating from the God of love. His very being, his very existence, exposed the idols of other people's lives for what they were, destructive tyrants. We are not told what happened to the man in the synagogue. The Gerasene demoniac goes home to his friends. Having come to terms with himself he is able to go and relate to others. The deaf and dumb boy is taken by the hand by Jesus who "lifted him up, and he arose" (Mark 9:27). Like the paralytic he too experienced a foretaste of resurrection. Jesus raises him up to a new, healed life.

Jesus' healing did not only manifest itself in the form of physical healings. He healed those who were marginalized and outcasts from society – those who hated themselves because others did, who considered themselves "evil", "sinners", "perverted", "unclean" or "riff-raff", because others had labelled them so. One of the things about Jesus that galled his opponents most was his habit of eating with "tax collectors and sinners" (Mark 2:16). Who were these people? People whose lives and occupations put them outside the Law. We know for instance that Jesus had friends and followers who were prostitutes. Tax collectors were despised by their fellow Jews for several reasons: firstly, because they worked for the Romans and their contact with Gentiles made them unclean; secondly, the fact that they worked for the occupying power made them collaborators; thirdly, they were known to be thoroughly fraudulent. In short, "sinners" were the sort of people that decent folk will cross the road to avoid, shady, undesirable characters. It is these people that Jesus sought out, not to preach at or to reform but to eat and drink with. In ancient Jewish society one only ate with one's closest friends. To invite someone to share a meal with you was to offer them deep friendship and intimacy. This makes Judas' betrayal of Jesus during a meal with him particularly poignant and treacherous. So the fact that Jesus chose to eat with "tax collectors and sinners" reveals that he identified with these people, he was one of them. He accepted such people without disapproval or condemnation and loved them unconditionally, thereby showing them that their lives were worth something in the eyes of God. He stood up for such people before those who were ready to dismiss them as inferior and condemn them (John 8:2–11). In God's kingdom, which he was seeking to establish, Jesus declared that all present values would be reversed: it was people such as these, the poor, despised and outcast, who would be given pride of place: "Truly, I say to you, the tax collectors and the harlots go into the kingdom of God before you" (Matthew 21:31), "But many that are first will be last, and the last first" (Matthew 19:30). This point is well illustrated in Jesus' attitude to women. In the society in which he lived women were not highly regarded. They were treated as the property of their fathers and husbands. Every day a Jewish man would thank God that he had not been made a woman because women were not permitted to read the Law and hence could not come near to God. Women were expected to be homemakers, bed partners and child rearers; they had little intrinsic value. Jesus broke all the rules. He seems to have deliberately sought out the company of women and counted them among his followers. He even talked theology with them (John 4:7–42 and Luke 10:38–42) and was prepared to be persuaded by their line of theological argument (Mark 7:24–30). Jesus treated women as his equals and in doing so showed them that God did not regard them as inferiors cut off from his Law. This was a radical attitude. Jesus gave women the chance to know and serve God. It was women who were the first to realize that God had raised Jesus from the dead and it was to women that he first appeared after the resurrection.

Jesus offered this healing, unconditional love to all. He came to set everyone on the road to wholeness/perfection: "You, therefore, must be perfect [*teleioi* = perfect or whole], as your heavenly father is perfect" (Matthew 5:48). Some, driven to despair by their brokenness, came to seek healing, or others came to seek it on their behalf. Others had to be offered that healing love before they could understand or acknowledge their brokenness. Zacchaeus, the tax collector, fits into this second category. He climbed into a tree simply to be able to watch Jesus pass by. But Jesus perceived the brokenness in him and his need for healing and offered it to him by insisting that he come and stay with Zacchaeus in his home. This display of spontaneous and unconditional love has an effect upon Zacchaeus that can only be described as "repentance". The word *metanoia* translated in the New Testament as "repent" means "turn around". In response to Jesus' love and acceptance Zacchaeus sees himself as he really is and turns himself around:

> And Zacchaeus stood and said to the Lord, "Behold, Lord, the half of my goods I give to the poor; and if I have defrauded any one of any-

thing, I restore it fourfold." And Jesus said to
him, "Today salvation has come to this house,
since he also is a son of Abraham. For the Son
of man came to seek and to save the lost."

Luke: 19:8–9

Others, however, rejected the offer of salvation that
Jesus brought, unable to acknowledge their brokenness and unwilling to take the risk of removing their
masks or losing their idols. Some members of the
Jewish religious authorities rejected Jesus's offer of
healing because they would not surrender the Law
which gave them authority, power and status in
society and justified their actions. The rich man of
Mark 10:17–22 cannot bring himself to reject his idol,
money. Jesus' own people, the people of Capernaum,
could not bring themselves to accept his unconditional
love and healing because their pride, their sense of
superiority, prevented them from acknowledging their
brokenness before a man they knew (Mark 6:1–6).
Jesus called people to a point of crisis, of decision, of
choice between authentic and inauthentic existence.

A question that immediately springs to mind when
studying those that Jesus healed is, "Did these people
continue to live healed, whole, unalienated lives until
their death or did they return to a state of brokenness?" There is nothing in the Gospels to suggest that
those whom Jesus healed did not later dissolve back
into pain and alienation. Lazarus and the son of the
widow of Nain had not been resurrected; they had to
face death a second time. The story of Jesus' death
and resurrection teaches us that only after complete

destruction can complete wholeness be experienced. Only death brings that complete destruction. What Jesus offered to those with whom he came into contact was a foretaste of the complete and everlasting wholeness that God was offering humankind, an offer that is confirmed in the resurrection of Jesus himself. In order to experience this foretaste of salvation all that was necessary was to acknowledge one's brokenness, to recognize how far one is from God and from one's neighbours. This is beautifully illustrated in the parable of the Pharisee and the tax collector:

> He also told this parable to some who trusted in themselves that they were righteous and despised others: "Two men went up into the temple to pray, one a Pharisee and the other a tax collector. The Pharisee stood and prayed thus with himself, 'God, I thank thee that I am not like other men, extortioners, unjust, adulterers, or even like this tax collector. I fast twice a week, I give tithes of all that I get.' But the tax collector, standing far off, would not even lift up his eyes to heaven, but beat his breast, saying, 'God, be merciful to me a sinner!' I tell you, this man went down to his house justified rather than the other; for everyone who exalts himself will be humbled, but he who humbles himself will be exalted." Luke 18:9–14

Familiarity with this parable can easily blind us to the radical claims Jesus is making in it. If we had been among those who had heard Jesus teaching this parable we would have been shocked to the core by his conclusion as to which one of the men was righteous before God. We would have been expecting Jesus to praise the Pharisee because he not only obeyed the Law but did so much more than the Law required. The tax collector, on the other hand, was a criminal and we would have considered his behaviour in the synagogue to be quite correct, he was after all a sinner. In contemporary terms it was as if Jesus was declaring that God preferred the company of a racketeering landlord to a saintly priest.

The point I believe Jesus was trying to draw his listeners' attention to in this parable is that the Pharisee refuses to face up to himself, refuses to acknowledge his brokenness. He has come to believe in his own masks. He has created two idols for himself, himself and the Law. Instead of treating the Law as a means to God, a signpost, he treats it as God. He uses the Law to protect himself from other people, to prevent himself from treating others as individual persons with dignity, needs and rights. He can dismiss the tax collector as a "sinner" and feel good about himself simply because he follows the letter of the Law to extremes. The Pharisee is blind to his own true self and to others and he is, although he does not realize it, blind to God. The tax collector, on the other hand, is painfully aware of his own broken condition, his enslavement to sin. He knows that he is alienated from God and from others and he knows that he is in need of salvation, and healing. This makes him open and ready to receive the healing grace of God. We all know people who, like Sam whom I mentioned in the first chapter, refuse to acknowledge their own brokenness, who steadfastly refuse to allow themselves to become vulnerable to hurt by loving, and who, for most of their lives, manage to avoid the sort of calamities that force people to wake up to their true selves. Such people skim along the surface of life and cannot understand or show real compassion to others wrestling with brokenness since they have no idea what they are going through. Such people are so distanced from the inner experience of their fellow beings that they almost cease to be human. As Theodore Robinson wrote,

> One who has suffered greatly is not necessarily better than he would otherwise have been, but his nature is certainly more complete. We cannot avoid the feeling that one who has never suffered would be incompletely human.[5]

Maggie is a mother of three and a fervent Roman Catholic. She brought all her children up as practising Catholics, sent them to Catholic schools and insisted that they attended Mass and all other devotions. She accepted without question all the Church's teaching. As her children reached puberty Maggie became obsessed with the fear that her children would fall into sin which at first she equated with neglecting to perform their religious duties. If one of her children stayed with a friend over a weekend Maggie would nag the child beforehand about the need to attend Mass and ring up to check that they had been. If the friend lived fairly locally Maggie would find an excuse to attend the church she supposed the friend's family would attend to check up on her offspring. When her children went to university she found out the Mass

times at the university chaplaincy and would tele-
phone her children's digs during those times to make
sure they were not there when they should be at Mass.

Maggie became equally obsessed with the children's sexual morality. When she had been a young
woman herself she had fallen in love with a man
somewhat older than herself who also happened to be
divorced. She had been tempted to sleep with this
man but her own mother's sophisticated surveillance
system prevented them! Her mother strongly disap-
proved of her boyfriend because he was divorced (a
sin in the eyes of the Church) and managed to per-
suade Maggie to end the relationship. Maggie eventually married a sensible, devout young Catholic. In her
heart of hearts Maggie was not happy in her marriage
and looked wistfully back to her first love and what
might have been. But she felt guilty and revolted with
herself for doing so and she suppressed her guilt and
unhappiness so that they became her shadow side.
She convinced herself that she was the happy mother
of an ideal Catholic family. Maggie was certain that
all her children, given the chance, would become
sexually immoral and she went to enormous lengths
to keep tabs on them and their relationships. She rang
them up in the middle of the night, grabbed the phone
when they were in the midst of conversations, forbade
them to go on holiday with members of the opposite
sex and ordered them to stop seeing certain people,
using money as a means of manipulation. Letters were
read, parents were rung, non-Catholics were kept
under special scrutiny. Maggie's obsession with her
own past and the rules of her faith prevented her from

accepting her children as responsible independent individuals. Instead she treated them like criminals who had to be kept upon the "straight and narrow".

Despite all her efforts, Maggie's two eldest children established extra-marital sexual relationships. They both loved their partners and were deeply committed to them. The elder child was quite naturally revolted by Maggie's obsession with religion and what she did in its name and for that reason no longer went to church. Maggie was distraught and disgusted with her children's behaviour. She refused to listen to their attempted explanations and simply cut herself off from her children by refusing to recognize the existence of their partners. She wrote them long letters pleading with them to turn away from their sin, to go to a priest and to come home. She continued to maintain that what she was doing was for their own good.

Maggie, like the Pharisee, refused to acknowledge her own brokenness. Also like the Pharisee she made the teaching of the Catholic Church into an idol that prevented her coming to know the loving, merciful, unjudging God proclaimed by Jesus. So frightened was she by her shadow side that she was determined that it should not manifest itself in her children. But she refused to acknowledge that she was in need of healing. In her eyes her children were nothing more than sinners. She could not allow herself to attempt to understand them lest she too got sucked back into the web of sin.

Little wonder that Jesus chose to socialize with those on the margins of society, those who had been rejected by their fellow human beings, those who knew already or were close to realizing they were in need of healing. Little wonder that he found himself in bitter conflict with those who refused to recognize their own brokenness but delighted in pointing out the brokenness of others. Such people found themselves threatened by Jesus' teaching which had the potential to subvert them.

What then does it mean to be healed, to be made whole, to be saved? It means to be loved. You suddenly realize that you are loved by God for what you are; bad bits, good bits and indifferent bits are all equally loved. Knowing that you are unconditionally loved by God can make you less hard on yourself, more able to cope with those things that make up the shadow side, less self-obsessed, less defensive, less insecure. With this revelation comes the realization that every human being is equally broken and equally precious in the eyes of the creator and loved with the same unconditional acceptance as yourself. Everyone deserves to be loved and respected as they are. A healed person is not alienated from those around them. He or she will be particularly aware of the personhood of those whom others treat as non-persons, the sort of person Jesus identified with. Healing is therefore a creative experience. Having received the transforming and liberating love of God yourself, you will want to take that love to others and make them aware of the possibility that this love brings. A healed person will not be judgemental but will fight for justice for the oppressed. He or she will seek to change the powers and institutions that depersonalize but a healed person will also recognize that as an individual before God he or she has no rights over others.

> Truly, I say to you, unless you turn and become like children, you will never enter the kingdom of heaven. Whoever humbles himself like this child, he is the greatest in the kingdom of heaven.
> Matthew 18:3–4

Usually this teaching of Jesus is interpreted in a very sentimental way. It is assumed that Jesus was holding children up as models of innocence and unquestioning minds. But the ancient Jews did not have such a sentimental view of children. In the Jewish society in which Jesus lived a child was regarded as a piece of property, it had no rights of its own. What Jesus wanted his disciples to realize was that we are all equal in the eyes of God, we are all at the bottom. So, just as Jesus identified with the non-persons of his time and as a result ended up a non-person himself, his disciples must risk being treated as people with no status. The teaching of the Sermon on the Mount spells this out in detail (Matthew 5–7).

I do not want to leave the impression that the life of Christ teaches us that brokenness, suffering, alienation and pain are good things because we need them to achieve salvation. The New Testament does not provide us with an intellectual explanation for the human condition. Jesus specifically refutes the belief of some of his contemporaries that physical suffering is punishment for past sin. John tells us that when Jesus was asked by his disciples whose sin had caused a man to be born blind, Jesus replied, "It was not that this man sinned, or his parents, but that the works of God might be made manifest in him" (John 9:3). No one was responsible for the man's blindness but God was ready to heal him because he knew he was in need of this.

St Paul accepted suffering as a sign and symptom of the fact that the universe is broken and incomplete but he also believed that Christ's resurrection had shown that such suffering could be seen as the first sign of the coming completeness, the birthpangs signalling the new life that was about to be born:

> I consider that the sufferings of this present time are not worth comparing with the glory that is to be revealed to us. For the creation waits with eager longing for the revealing of the sons of God; for the creation was subjected to futility, not of its own will but by the will of him who subjected it in hope; because creation itself will be set free from its bondage to decay and obtain the glorious liberty of the children of God. We know that the whole creation has been groaning in travail together until now; and not only the creation, but we ourselves, who have the first fruits of the Spirit, groan inwardly as we wait for adoption as sons, the redemption of our bodies.
>
> Romans 8:18–23

The sufferings of the human condition are not explained or glorified by either Jesus or Paul. They are just acknowledged to exist and made the starting point for the process of salvation.

77

God became human in Jesus Christ. God entered
the human condition completely and unconditionally.
During his life he showed those who knew they were
broken by life what wholeness and healing were like,
he showed them by loving them. Loving makes you
vulnerable to hurt and rejection and God was completely destroyed by being human. He died a horrific,
painful death and was propelled by the inhumanity
of those whom he had tried to love into the abyss of
annihilation. But out of this complete and utter end
came a completely new beginning. God resurrected
himself in Christ from death and nothingness into a
new, healed life. As Paul put it:

> But in fact Christ has been raised from the dead,
> the first fruits of those who have fallen asleep.
> For as by a man came death, by a man has come
> also the resurrection of the dead. For as in Adam
> all die, so also in Christ shall all be made alive.
>
> 1 Corinthians 15:20–2

The next question we have to tackle is how do *we*
come to participate in that whole and healed life that
God has created in Christ?

3

Transforming Grace

By his broken body,
we, the body of humanity,
are made whole,
whoever we are and wherever we are,
whatever our doubts or shame,
our turmoil or anger.
We are healed and can come together
in the fullness of the Body of Christ.

He has penetrated into the depths of darkness,
loneliness, rejection, agony and fear,
in order to touch the depths of darkness
in each one of us
and to call us to belief,
to call us to walk in this world of darkness,
loneliness, rejection, agony and fear –
hoping, trusting in the resurrection.[1]

God incarnate in Jesus Christ offered a foretaste of
his kingdom, of complete wholeness, to those with
whom he came into contact during his earthly life.
After his death he resurrected himself to a completely
new type of existence, a completely healed existence.
How might those who come after Christ, who live in

the post-resurrection era, experience the same glimpses of wholeness in their lives as did the demoniacs, lepers, paralytics and sinners of Christ's day? How can we become incorporated into Christ's resurrection from the dead so that we too are raised from complete destruction to complete wholeness?

St Paul seems to have been the first Christian theologian to attempt to answer this question. Like us, Paul did not meet Jesus of Nazareth while he was alive and yet Paul was convinced that Christ's resurrection was an "incorporative" event, that is, all men and women participated in it. His answer as to how can be summed up in one word – grace. The origin of the concept of grace developed by Paul can be traced back to the Old Testament. A common theme running throughout the Old Testament but found with most frequency in the Psalms is God's favour (in Hebrew *hen*) to Israel. God shows his favour, or good will, to his people by delivering them from things that threaten them, despite the fact that they consistently break their side of the covenant with God:

> Be gracious to me, O Lord!
> Behold what I suffer from those who hate me,
> O thou who liftest me up from the gates of death,
> that I may recount all thy praises,
> that in the gates of the daughter of Zion
> I may rejoice in thy deliverance. Psalm 9:13–14

> As for me, I said, "O Lord, be gracious to me;
> heal me, for I have sinned against thee!"
> Psalm 41:4

> And he said, "I will make all my goodness pass
> before you, and will proclaim before you my
> name 'The Lord'; and I will be gracious to whom
> I will be gracious, and will show mercy on whom
> I will show mercy." Exodus 33:19

In the New Testament it is the Greek word *charis* that
is translated as "grace" in the English versions. In
Paul's epistles it carries the same meaning as the
Hebrew *hen* – a free gift from God. Paul develops this
idea; for him it is the gift of deliverance from the
sinful condition of the human race (Romans 5:15),
deliverance from slavery to the Law (Romans 6:14),
to sin and to death (Romans 6:9–11), and incorporation into the new, eternal life of the risen Christ.

> The end of those things [sin] is death. But now that
> you have been set free from sin and have become
> slaves of God, the return you get is sanctification
> and its end, eternal life. For the wages of sin is
> death, but the free gift *(charisma)* of God is eternal
> life in Christ Jesus our Lord. Romans 6:21–3

Paul often links grace with peace. The Hebrew concept of peace *(shalom)* includes not only harmony and
a state of non-antagonism and non-hostility but also
health, welfare, justice and right order. Peace was
regarded as the essential characteristic of the kingdom
that was to be established by the Messiah, the saviour
awaited by the Jews – so much so that it became a
synonym for the Messianic kingdom:

> How beautiful upon the mountains
> are the feet of him who brings good tidings,

who publishes peace, who brings good tidings of
    good,
who publishes salvation,
who says to Zion, "Your God reigns."

                                 Isaiah 52:7

Which is why Luke has the heavenly host proclaim
"Glory to God in the highest, and on earth *peace*
among men with whom he is pleased" (Luke 2:14) at
the birth of Jesus the Messiah.

Grace is also closely linked to forgiveness in the
writings of Paul and his disciples:

> And you, who were dead in trespasses and the
> uncircumcision of your flesh, God made alive
> together with him, having forgiven (*charisamenos*)
> us all our trespasses.   Colossians 2:13

For Paul, then, "grace" is simply a word to describe
the Christian conviction that God gave himself unconditionally to humanity in order to heal it. The cross
on which hangs a man reviled and murdered by his
fellow human beings is the supreme statement of
God's love for humanity. Men and women destroy
themselves, just as they destroyed God in Christ, and
yet God loves them unconditionally and out of their
destruction raises indestructibility, out of their brokenness he raises wholeness, out of their finitude he
raises eternal life; human nature is perfected and in
that perfection transformed.

The early Church Fathers interpreted grace as a
process of divinization; as a process whereby human
beings became divine. On the one hand, this was

undoubtedly a legitimate development of the teaching of the New Testament that Christ was raised to a new type of existence which Paul calls "spiritual", very different from the broken existence of most of humanity. But, on the other hand, those who thought of grace in terms of divinization tended to take a very negative view of human nature, regarding it as corrupt and depraved, the very opposite of divinity; salvation was seen as a means of escape from human nature. St Augustine has been dubbed the "Doctor of Grace" because it was he who worked out a theology of it. His personal experience of life convinced him that human nature was so depraved and weak, as a result of Adam's fall from God, that men and women could not perform a single good work without the aid of grace. Like all the early Church Fathers, Augustine tended to talk about grace as if it were some sort of divine energy infused into the human soul to transform it. The theologians of the Reformation took an even lower view of humanity than the early Church Fathers. The Swiss Reformer John Calvin could even go as far as to assert that God hated humankind because of its sinfulness.

There are many reasons for rejecting this understanding of grace as unsatisfactory. It gives the impression that grace is something distinct from God, a divine fluid that God chooses to pour into those he has specially selected, predestined, to be saved, enabling them to start climbing the ladder that leads to divinization – the divine equivalent of Esso Supergrade motor oil. These predestined people become super-people and the ideal super-person for Augustine and for many other early theologians was one who suppressed and denied great chunks of their humanity, all the elements considered likely to drag a person down into depravity. Augustine identified concupiscence – selfish desire, particularly sexual desire – with the original sin of Adam that taints all men and women and prevents them from being able to resist sin. Augustine showed great perception in realizing that human beings are incapable of achieving salvation through their own efforts without the help of God. We are trapped in our own brokenness and despair and cannot hope to attain wholeness without the help of a healer. Yet, not only does this idea of grace as something poured into certain people undermine humankind's freedom to accept or reject God's grace, making life a cruel and pointless farce in which we are all helplessly predestined to either eternal salvation or damnation, but it also contradicts experience. Millions of people are born and die without ever coming to know God and yet it would be ridiculous to assert that such people never experience a moment of wholeness and unalienated communion with another person nor do a single good act. Think of people who are mentally ill. They will often be capable of acting in a sane manner at times, even though they will still be suffering from mental illness. Similarly, however broken and alienated from God people might be, they are still able to experience brief glimpses of salvation. Furthermore, is there any evidence that God wants us to become super-persons and transcend all selfish desire, especially sexual desire? We have observed that when God chose to come among humanity he came not as a super-person but as an ordinary human being subject to the same desires, concerns and temptations as you or I. He died as broken by life as any other human being and was raised to new life still bearing the marks of human existence. All this should make it clear to us that God came not to deliver us from our humanity but to save our humanity, to heal it by delivering it from the sources of brokenness. Christianity has been guilty of missing the point of the incarnation almost from the start, by making Jesus into a super-person, devoid of sin and concupiscence. The fact that none of the New Testament writers draw attention to Jesus' sexuality might suggest that there was nothing worth remarking upon – he experienced the same emotions as everyone else. What we can conclude from the portrait painted by the evangelists is that Jesus would have fought against the temptation to treat anyone merely as an object to be used to satisfy his own desire.

The Church Fathers' reluctance to believe that God could love humanity or bear to enter into it fully and unconditionally is understandable, bogged down as it is in squalid sin and hell-bent on self-destruction. If I were God I wouldn't do it! Here lies the rub. It is a constant temptation for Christians to assume that God is like us in the sense that he shares our values, morality, and ethic, and so we feel quite confident in speaking on behalf of God and pronouncing judgement on certain issues in his name. A quick glance at the Gospels, however, should be enough to dispel this illusion. The God that Jesus reveals is a God who is not worried about his own rights or having justice

done to him. He is the prodigal father who runs out
to greet his errant son, who will not listen to his
prepared speech of regret, who doesn't sulk or lecture
him, who doesn't make his son do some sort of penance, nor compare him unfavourably with the son
who has stayed at home, but lays on a huge feast
instead (Luke 15:11–32)! He is a God who prefers the
company of sinners and losers to that of the righteous
and successful and doesn't care what other people
think of him. He is a God who refuses to treat women
and children as other people's property but regards
them as full persons. He is a God who asks those who
would be like him not to judge others (Matthew
7:1–2) nor strike back at those who hurt them (Matthew 5:38–9). He is a God who asks those who would
be like him to be weak, disadvantaged and powerless.
He is a God concerned only with the needs and rights
of others (Matthew 25:31–46). This is indeed a God
very, very different from us!

I am, of course, laying myself wide open to the
charge of having done what I have accused the
Church Fathers of doing, reading into God my own
concerns and preoccupations. As one of my more
forthright students remarked after one of my lectures
on the suffering of God, "The trouble with your God,
Liz, is that he is just like you!" For years I accepted
the traditional concepts of God, Christ and salvation
that I have described earlier. I can remember the day
when I began seriously to question them. It was the
day I finished reading Harry Williams' autobiography, *Some Day I'll Find You*. Williams' account of how
he wrestled with the God of the Christian tradition,

the God of justice who hated sin and sacrificed his sinless son to redeem mankind, the God who wanted us to become super-people, until the struggle crushed and broke his spirit so horrified me that I was shocked into the realization that the God who is preached from the pulpit is more often than not the creation of the pulpit and is a caricature of the God revealed by Christ. As Voltaire put it, "God created man and man returned the compliment". The pulpit God is powerful and all knowing, he is the God of hierarchy and judgement, he is a comfortable, predictable God, he is humanity writ large. But as the great twentieth-century theologian Karl Barth pointed out, you don't say "God" simply by saying "Humanity" in a loud voice. The God revealed by Christ chooses to be powerless, he champions those at the bottom and threatens those at the top. He is a very uncomfortable God, to be found in the most unlikely people and places. He cannot be tied down and packaged up but blows where he wills. It is therefore my reluctant conclusion that down the centuries Christians have had a tendency to misunderstand the reality of the incarnation, the humanity of Christ and the nature of grace. Grace is not a divine energy, it is a person. Grace is God revealed by Christ. As Richard McBrien has put it,

> "Grace" is essentially God's self-communication to us men and women, and, secondarily, the effect(s) of that self-communication.[2]

God communicates himself to us through Jesus Christ; he communicates his desire to save us and the nature of the salvation offered through his resurrection and he gives us the possibility of entering into a healing relationship with him. As Paul realized, salvation is offered not just to a few but to all: "He who did not spare his own Son but gave him up for us all" (Romans 8:32); "For as in Adam all die, so also in Christ shall all be made alive" (1 Corinthians 15:22). We can choose to enter into a relationship with God and experience something of the wholeness that will be ours beyond this life or we can choose not to. Are we to conclude, as for centuries the majority of Christians have done, that those who do not know God, either through choice or circumstance or "heretical" misinterpretation, will be unable to share in the resurrection? The God revealed by Christ is a God who rejects no one. He is a God who has been human and who therefore understands the obstacles to knowledge of God. He knows what it is to feel totally alone in the universe and to give up trusting in himself. All are equally loved by God – the parable told by Jesus of the workers in the vineyard makes this very plain:

> For the kingdom of heaven is like a householder who went out early in the morning to hire labourers for his vineyard. After agreeing with the labourers for a denarius a day, he sent them into his vineyard. And going out about the third hour he saw others standing idle in the market place; and to them he said, "You go into the vineyard too, and whatever is right I will give you.' So they went. Going out again about the sixth hour and the ninth hour, he did the same. And about

the eleventh hour he went out and found others standing; and he said to them, "Why do you stand here idle all day?" They said to him, "Because no one has hired us." He said to them, "You go into the vineyard too." And when evening came, the owner of the vineyard said to his steward, "Call the labourers and pay them their wages, beginning with the last, up to the first." And when those hired about the eleventh hour came, each of them received a denarius. Now when the first came, they thought they would receive more; but each of them also received a denarius. And on receiving it they grumbled at the householder, saying, "These last worked only one hour, and you have made them equal to us who have borne the burden of the day and the scorching heat." But he replied to one of them, "Friend, I am doing you no wrong; did you not agree with me for a denarius? Take what belongs to you, and go; I choose to give to this last as I give to you. Am I not allowed to do what I choose with what belongs to me? Or do you begrudge my generosity?" So the last will be first, and the first last. Matthew 20:1–16

Like those who laboured all day we might find it very unfair and unjust that those who live evil and immoral lives are destined for the same gift from God as we are. I was recently at a church service where the preacher argued that God has a special love and concern for his disciples. "What sort of God", he asked, "would love Hitler as much as he loves you?" I resisted the urge to stand up and yell back, "The God of the New Testament". From the perspective of broken human nature God's love for sinners is unfair and unjust, because we convince ourselves that we are "superior" to others, but that is the price we pay for a God who judges no one and we will be very grateful for such a God when it finally dawns on us that we are all at the bottom of the ladder, all as broken as each other.

So if we are all to partake in the resurrection eventually why bother to come to know God in this life and take on board the considerable demands that the Gospel makes upon us? There are two reasons why it is preferable that we should know God in this life: firstly, in order to know some real wholeness and healing and realize that these all too brief flashes of wholeness are a foretaste of what is to come. We can therefore live our lives in hope.

The second reason is that such knowledge of God makes sense of our lives, because we are given a task to perform. In the synoptic Gospels (Matthew, Mark and Luke) Jesus says surprisingly little about life after death. His principal concern is to establish the kingdom of God on earth. Confident of the coming resurrection his followers should not be preoccupied with their own eternal destiny but concern themselves with creating a society appropriate to humanity's status as "Easter people", people destined for a new, healed existence. Christ calls for a society based upon love, not greed, where the hungry are fed, the poor provided for, where no one is marginalized or rejected, where no one lords it over another and where no one is depersonalized; a society where God's salvation, his *shalom*, can be made manifest at least to a partial degree. Things will never be perfect, not in this existence, but they can be better. Christianity is not about "pie in the sky when you die". It is about fighting against the forces of depersonalization to affirm the personhood of each and every individual on this planet. Whoever started the rumour that Christianity is not a political faith got the wrong end of the stick. It is not only political, it is revolutionary, for it seeks to turn the world upside down and ensure that those who are now last – the poor, sick, homeless and oppressed – will be first. A Christian will not be other-worldly, he or she will look for God in the challenge that God is presenting us with in this world.

It is by grace that we are incorporated into the saving work of Christ. The Church teaches that this grace is mediated to us through the *sacraments*. At the mention of the word "sacrament" most Christians will think of the ritual ceremonies known as baptism, the eucharist or communion and perhaps other rites like confirmation and marriage. We are going to look at these rites in some detail in the next chapter. For the moment I want to look at the notion of sacrament in the broadest possible terms.

Christians believe that God is the creator of this world and that he loves it so much that he chose to enter into it as a human being and share both its beauty and its horror. God chose to reveal himself through a finite being, through part of his creation. Although God communicates himself most clearly through the man, Jesus of Nazareth, it follows that, since he is the author of all creation, he can reveal himself through any part of it. The Old Testament bears witness to this: Moses became aware of something of the reality and nature of God through a burning bush (Exodus 3:2–6). The prophet Elijah sought God in a gale, an earthquake and fire but only encountered God in a "still small voice", a gentle breeze (1 Kings 19:11–12). The whole of reality has the potential to reveal the nature of God and thus has the potential to be a sacrament. A sacrament is simply a finite instrument through which we can perceive something of the nature of the infinite, the divine. It is also an instrument through which God communicates his healing love. As McBrien has noted, the term "sacramental" can be applied,

> to any finite reality through which the divine is perceived to be disclosed and communicated, and through which our human response to the divine assumes some measure of shape, form, and structure.[3]

Let me try and elucidate by offering a few examples. I noted in chapter one that one of the clearest manifestations of human brokenness is physical or mental illness. Broadly speaking, serious illness can have one of two effects upon the person concerned: it can make them bitter, introverted and angry with God and with those around them or it can bring home with enormous force a person's brokenness and this makes them open and ready to receive God's healing grace. Luke's portrait of the two criminals crucified with Jesus illustrates these two reactions beautifully:

> One of the criminals who were hanged railed at him, saying, "Are you not the Christ? Save yourself and us!" But the other rebuked him, saying, "Do you not fear God, since you are under the same sentence of condemnation? And we indeed justly; for we are receiving the due reward of our deeds; but this man has done nothing wrong." And he said, "Jesus, remember me when you come into your kingdom." And he said to him, "Truly, I say to you, today you will be with me in Paradise." Luke 23:39–43

For those who are able to use their illness and pain to face up to their brokenness, illness can become a sacrament through which the person who is ill comes to realize that God is not a God who rescues his beloved from pain but is a God who can be found in pain and helplessness, since he too has been tormented by incessant pain and it is out of that pain and helplessness that he rose to a healed, healthy life. In *Facing Illness* (Epworth Press, 1986), Nigel Collinson and David Matthews draw a deeply moving comparison between a patient handed over to a hospital, who thus becomes a stranger in the midst of strangers and stripped of his independence, and Jesus who was handed over to strangers by Judas, one of his closest friends, and changed from doing to being done to, from action to passion. They point out that it was as patient, as someone who has to wait for others to do things for and to him, that Jesus most clearly and truly revealed God. If a patient realizes that God shares in the suffering and pain of humanity, the realization can lead to a fleeting experience of healing and resurrection, in the ability, for perhaps a few moments only, to rise above the illness, to see beyond it.

When wrestling with the problem of pain C. S. Lewis concluded,

> God whispers to us in our pleasures, speaks in our conscience, but shouts in our pains. It is his megaphone to rouse a deaf world.[4]

God's voice cannot only be heard in pain by the suffering person; patients themselves can become sacramental. Some time ago I found myself in a medical ward of the local hospital. I was in severe pain that ate away my strength and resilience. All the other ladies who shared my section of the ward were also in severe pain or discomfort. As time went on I began to notice that at least once each day one of us became very low in spirits, introverted and weepy. When this happened the other women would allow the unhappy person space to be alone with their grief and then exactly at the right moment one or other of them would offer a word or gesture that would communicate the fact they knew exactly what you were going through and that although they could not offer any glib answers they could offer love and support. These almost imperceptible gestures would bring a temporary relief from inner brokenness to the person concerned. There was one lady in particular whom I shall never forget. Dolly was very unwell. She was diabetic,

nearly blind, had heart trouble, high blood pressure
– you name it, she had it. She was also a very large
lady weighing in at around twenty-five stone. She
hated being ill and in pain, and like all of us on the
ward, had some very dark moments, but she had a
remarkable ability to transcend her own illness and
take others with her. She loved people and she loved
life which she regarded as a humorous adventure. She
had us all weeping with laughter as she told us stories,
often against herself, of her life so that we too tran-
scended our physical and mental pain and met together at a different level, a level of mutual acceptance
and love. All the ladies, but especially Dolly, became
sacraments of God's healing love for me and enabled
me to experience something of the joy and peace of
the resurrection in a time of great pain, turmoil and
brokenness.

In his latest book Harry Williams argues that
laughter is both a sign and a medium of God's grace:

> God, we believe, accepts us, accepts all men,
> unconditionally, warts and all. Laughter is the
> purest form of our response to God's acceptance
> of us. For when I laugh at myself I accept myself
> and when I laugh at other people in genuine
> mirth I accept them. Self-acceptance in laughter
> is the very opposite of self-satisfaction or pride.
> For in laughter I accept myself not because I'm
> some sort of super-person, but precisely because
> I'm not. There is nothing funny about a super-
> person. There is everything funny about a man
> who thinks he is. In laughing at my own claims

95

to importance or regard I receive myself in a sort
of loving forgiveness which is an echo of God's
forgiveness of me.[5]

There is a great deal of humour in Jesus' teaching. I
didn't realize this until I heard the actor Alec
McCowen giving his famous rendition of Mark's
Gospel and found myself roaring with laughter at
some of the parables and parts of the Sermon on the
Mount. He brought out beautifully the way in which
Jesus made piety and self-satisfaction look positively
ridiculous. Those who acknowledged their brokenness
could laugh at themselves; those who refused to found
his teasing threatening.

During my time in hospital I witnessed a great
deal of unchristian behaviour. I observed doctors who
treated patients more like slides under a microscope
than human beings. They would march in, adorned
in white coats, surrounded by an entourage of junior
doctors and nurses, the embodiment of unapproach-
able authority. Some did not even condescend to
speak to the person lying before them but stood at
the foot of the bed asking questions of the other doctors, only approaching the patient to pull back the
blanket and poke about at the flesh. These doctors
hid themselves behind a mask of professional com-
petence and authority. It was a common grouse
amongst patients that their consultants behaved as if
they were God. These doctors were afraid to take
the risk of removing the mask, of making themselves
vulnerable and meeting their patients on an equal
level, lest they be questioned, their ignorance or

insecurity exposed, or lest the patient became upset and emotional and in need of more than medical expertise, in need of compassion, in need of personal involvement. As a consequence they were totally alienated from their patients who were left angry, confused and, above all, worried and therefore not in a condition conducive to recovery.

I also saw visitors who, while they might have meant well, demonstrated quite remarkable insensitivity towards their friends and loved ones. Some simply refused to talk about the patient's condition even when the patient was in a great deal of discomfort or very afraid and upset. These people tried to cheer the patient up with anecdotes which centred almost entirely upon themselves. Others were more than generous with reassurance, advice and tales of people who had suffered similar complaints, when it was obvious to the patient that there were, in fact, no grounds for such effusive assurance. Others were positively antagonistic towards the patient, irritated by their illness, trying to encourage them to "pull themselves together", stop being so weak and sorry for themselves and blaming the patient's physical discomfort on their mental state. All these visitors were evidently afraid of illness but not primarily on behalf of the patient but for themselves. They did not want to face up to their own brokenness and finitude so they either avoided the topic of illness altogether or pretended that it was not as serious as it was, or they became angry with the patient for manifesting human brokenness in such an unavoidable manner.

However, I was also privileged to observe behaviour on the part of visitors and doctors which became sacramental for me and for others. Some visitors created the kind of atmosphere in which patients felt free to express the fear, anger, pain, humiliation and helplessness that they were experiencing, either through words, tears or silent communication, and they offered no false reassurance nor cheerful advice. All these visitors offered to the patient was their own helplessness, their own fear and their own brokenness, so that the patients understood that they were not alone in their struggle, one person at least was standing with them. All this might be expressed in something as simple as a hand clasped or an arm stroked. All this could be sacramental because it could convey the acceptance, love, understanding and compassion that God offers humankind, which enables the sick person to see beyond sickness to a new, healed existence. Remember Jesus' treatment of sick people. He went straight to the deepest concerns and needs of the patient and indicated through words or action that God understood, he cared deeply and loved unconditionally. A sensitive and compassionate visitor can bring the patient temporary knowledge of healing and wholeness simply by listening, loving and understanding. They may not know it but they become instruments through which God mediates his healing love and presence.

I was very lucky to be under the care of a consultant rheumatologist whose attitude to his patients was startlingly different from those doctors who appeared to suffer from delusions of divinity. Dr H. never appeared at the end of his patients' beds wearing a white coat or surrounded by a pack of junior doctors. He would always appear either alone or with one junior doctor (whom he would ignore) and would draw up a chair so that he could meet the patient on equal terms. One day when I was sitting in a chair on the ward he came and knelt beside me. When you are used to being towered over by people who have come to do things to you such a gesture means a great deal. Dr H. would come and see patients who had taken a turn for the worse, or become upset, at times when another consultant would have sent a junior. He would listen and comfort not only with words but with simple physical gestures. He always spoke directly to patients, explaining their condition and the treatment he was considering giving them and encouraged them to ask questions and express worries and doubts, allowing them to take decisions about their own treatment. Above all he was honest and ready to admit when he simply did not know an answer to a question. In my own case there were several months when he simply did not know what was wrong with me. Whereas others would have either dismissed me as a neurotic woman with whom there was nothing physically wrong or tried to disguise their ignorance by blinding me with medical science, Dr H. treated me and all his patients as persons whose dignity, rights and opinions had to be respected and guarded. He showed that he understood what it is like to be trapped in a prison of pain and he gave the impression that he cared for the person more than the disease. Of course, it is a very risky business to admit that you do not know and to make yourself approachable by those whom you are trying to cure; patients can get angry and abusive and reject you. I am not trying to portray this doctor as some sort of saint (and he would no doubt be appalled if I was). He was very human in his irritation with junior doctors and with patients who refused to cooperate with him and above all with the bureaucracy of the hospital and the NHS. I do not know whether he is a Christian but it was through his attitude to his patients that I came to understand a little better Christ's attitude to the people he came into contact with. When you become ill, and particularly when the illness manifests itself in physical symptoms such as, in my case, difficulty in walking, people start to treat you as "disabled" and they feel free to push and literally shove you about, shout at you as though you are deaf and address you as if you are mentally impaired. It is a very depressing experience. Therefore, to be treated as an equal, intelligent person, with understanding, respect and concern, by the person who knows most about your condition and whose care you are in is not only a great relief, it can also have a healing effect.

On one occasion Dr H. turned to me and said, "You should be angry with me for not having got your pain under control". This doctor inviting me to be angry with him suddenly made me realize that God too invites us to vent our anger upon him. As most people now know, it is necessary to express anger if we want to be healthy, but many people still bottle up their anger with others, with the state of the society and world in which they live and with themselves. It can eat away at their personality, turning it bitter and sour, and if anger is expressed towards others it often simply provokes further anger which eventually explodes into destructive violence. Anger that is not returned but is responded to with love can be the first step towards wholeness because it can be the first acknowledgement of one's brokenness.

Being in hospital, absorbed by my own illness and involved in other people's illness, made me realize how easy it would be to get to a point where one doesn't want to be healed because of the responsibilities and risks that being a healthy person involves. Sick people can often wield enormous power over their loved ones, power that they would not be afforded if they were well. A sick person needs large amounts of love and concern but can receive these without feeling any duty to give any back. A sick person can assume sickness as a mask to hide behind, to avoid the conflict between wholeness and brokenness.

Now there is in Jerusalem by the Sheep Gate a pool, in Hebrew called Beth-zatha, which has five porticoes. In these lay a multitude of invalids, blind, lame, paralysed. One man was there, who had been ill for thirty-eight years. When Jesus saw him and knew that he had been lying there a long time, he said to him, "Do you want to be healed?" The sick man answered him, "Sir, I have no man to put me into the pool when the water is troubled, and while I am going another steps down before me." Jesus said to him, "Rise, take up your pallet, and walk." And at once the man was healed, and he took up his pallet and walked.

Now that day was the sabbath. So the Jews said to the man who was cured, "It is the sabbath, it is not lawful for you to carry your pallet." But he answered them, "The man who healed me said to me, 'Take up your pallet, and walk.' " They asked him, "Who is the man who said to you, 'Take up your pallet, and walk?' " Now the man who had been healed did not know who it was, for Jesus had withdrawn, as there was a crowd in the place. Afterward, Jesus found him in the temple, and said to him, "See, you are well! Sin no more, that nothing worse befall you." The man went away and told the Jews that it was Jesus who had healed him. And this was why the Jews persecuted Jesus, because he did this on the sabbath. John 5:2–16

The subject of this healing story is a perfect example of a person who had lost the will to be well. He had got used to being a disabled person and feared the prospect of a healed existence. Jesus realizes this immediately and challenges the man as to whether he actually wants to be well. Notice that the man does not answer "Yes, of course I do", as one would perhaps expect. Nor does he answer "No, I don't", which might have been the honest reply but would have lost him the chance of sympathy from others. Instead he starts to blame others for the fact that he has not been healed although he has been sitting by the healing waters for a long time. By challenging the man Jesus exposes the root of the man's problems, he has become comfortable with his own brokenness. It is this exposure that heals the man, that raises him up to a new healed existence. Immediately, the man finds himself in just the sort of situation which as a paralytic he had been able to avoid and feared. People start questioning his actions, expecting explanations. Notice that these people do not see the man, all they see is a "sinner", someone who has broken the Law by carrying his bed on the Sabbath. Their distorted allegiance to the Law has blinded them to the needs and concerns of individuals and is preventing them from experiencing the love of God that would liberate them from slavery to the Law. This story also clearly illustrates the very temporary nature of any healing experienced during this life. The healed man, after having been questioned by the opponents of Jesus, cannot cope with condemnation by those in power and the risk to his own safety and falls back into brokenness, into putting himself before others, even if that means putting the other person at risk.

As I pointed out earlier, having experienced healing oneself one cannot just sit back and bask in one's wholeness: healing is creative. Like a healed paralytic we have to stand up and walk against those who refuse to recognize their own brokenness and who marginalize and depersonalize others. We must stand with the marginalized and depersonalized, bring them God's love and acceptance. In other words healing involves becoming sacraments. This is, as the man in John 5 quickly finds out, a risky business and one can find oneself under attack and withdrawing back into selfish concern, but the call, the responsibility, is always there in the eyes of the hungry, wounded, displaced, jobless, poverty-stricken and unloved.

People who take a stand against oppression, injustice and marginalization will often become unconscious sacraments of God's healing grace. When I was younger I spent a couple of weeks during the summer helping out at the East End Mission in London. Here homeless men and women, unmarried mothers, and women who had been the victims of violence were offered shelter, food, clothes and, if they wanted it, help to reintegrate into society. I saw dignity restored to people who had been rejected by their families, friends and society, and who often found themselves trapped in a web of deception, alcohol, drugs, violence and crime which made them despise themselves. The restoration came about simply because they were treated as people who deserved respect. They were not patronized nor harangued. They were not expected to be grateful for the food, clothing and counselling offered. They were given the time and space to be themselves and to express their anger and sadness and they were offered understanding. If they chose to go out and get drunk, returning to cause a rumpus and vomit all over the place, they were not told off like naughty children but cleaned up and understood. People who had been homeless for twenty years or more were given the confidence to move into a house with several others and take on the responsibility of running a home. Women who had been subject to the most horrific physical and mental abuse were given the love and respect that enabled them to re-enter the community and risk forming new relationships. All the residents were educated about their rights and entitlements and were given help and advice on how to take advantage of them. The staff were always ready to fight against the stone face of the system for the rights of the residents. They also found themselves battling against local and national government over issues such as the provision of housing, level of benefits, training schemes and so on. The care that they demonstrated for those on the edges of society was creative and healing but it also involved conflict and risk.

In chapter two we examined the healing Jesus brought to a leper, one of the most feared and marginalized people in ancient Israelite society. In modern Western society leprosy has been largely eradicated but in recent years a disease has come to light which is feared with the same violent, intense fear as leprosy was and whose victims are treated with the same hysterical rejection and fear as the lepers of biblical times. That disease is, of course, Acquired Immune Deficiency Syndrome.

When news of AIDS first permeated the public consciousness it produced a gross overreaction. Suddenly people became wary of drinking from the same cup as another person; rumours abounded as to how easy it was to catch AIDS; hairdressers, hospitals, cafés, swimming pools became potential death traps. People began to think twice about going to the aid of an accident victim, prison officers demanded protective clothing. Some began to call for the isolation of

AIDS victims. Then we began to hear of AIDS sufferers or their relatives being sacked from their work. Children who had become infected with the antibodies through the transfusion of contaminated blood were taunted and rejected by their school fellows. Homosexuals already banished to the margins of society for loving people of the same sex became objects of even greater fear, hate and intolerance and were made the scapegoats, the ones on whom blame for the disease was laid. Homosexuals who were diagnosed HIV positive often found themselves not only facing death but facing it alone, rejected by those closest to them because their families and friends could only see the disease and the label "homosexual" and could not see the person underneath. Some who claim to be followers of Christ declared that the disease proved that God found homosexuality an abomination.

In the autumn of 1987 I watched a television programme entitled "Aids: A Priest's Testimony". It dealt with the work of Father Bernard Lynch, an Irish missionary priest who chose to work among the homosexual community in New York. In these people so despised and rejected by society who could yet manifest such love and devotion towards one another, Father Lynch encountered Christ. He recognized God's presence in their love and witnessed the healing it brought. In turn, Father Lynch, by his acceptance and love of these people and in particular his spiritual ministrations to those dying with AIDS and their partners, brought God's healing grace to them, many of whom had been driven from the Church by its blanket condemnation of active homosexuals as sinners. As a result of Father Lynch's ministry much of the bitterness, hate and anger these people felt towards society and the Church evaporated and was replaced by a creative desire to help others to understand by loving them. At the end of this very moving programme it was revealed that Father Lynch had been removed from New York and sent to Rome. The reason given was that the Vatican felt that his work contravened the ruling that priests are not to give any encouragement to active homosexuals except to call them to renounce their sin. As this message rolled off the screen I was reminded of those opponents of Jesus who tried to scupper his ministry simply because he would not obey the rules and because he proclaimed that God loved people more than laws. People who seek to control the flow of God's grace, claiming that it only falls on those who are willing to submit to their power, and do so in Christ's name, are in danger of being guilty of blasphemy.

Father Lynch had to pay a price for being a sacrament of God's grace and so did his homosexual friends. This is something we have noted over and over again in our examination of God's healing grace. The twentieth-century theologian Dietrich Bonhoeffer put it well when he argued that there was no such thing as "cheap grace", grace that is received but which requires nothing from the recipient. On the contrary, all grace is "costly grace":

Such grace is *costly* because it calls us to follow, and it is *grace* because it calls us to follow *Jesus*

Christ. It is costly because it costs man his life, and it is grace because it gives a man the only true life.[6]

Indeed, for Bonhoeffer grace did cost him his life as he felt that it called him, along with several contemporaries, to speak out against the Nazi regime in his German homeland. On 9 April 1945 he was executed for his part in a plot to assassinate Hitler and engineer a military coup.

Grace is costly because, initially, it involves confronting one's own brokenness, which can be a very painful experience, and then taking sides with the powerless, divesting yourself of power and becoming as vulnerable as they. It involves entering their pain, hurt, anger and confusion, entering their brokenness and transforming them with God's unconditional love. It involves becoming a voice for those kept voiceless and a target for the oppressor.

Jean Vanier, a former professor of philosophy, felt called by grace to establish L'Arche, a community of people with mental handicaps and their assistants near Paris, where all are loved and cared for as individual persons and allowed the dignity which is theirs by right as creatures of God. They look after each other, run workshops together and spend part of every day in prayer together. L'Arche communities have now spread to many countries, including Britain. Vanier feels that by sharing the lives of people with mental handicaps he and his assistants are simply following Christ by bringing God's healing grace to those who need it most. People with mental handicaps have also been a source of grace for Vanier himself:

> The poor and the weak have revealed to me
> the great secret of Jesus.
> If you wish to follow him
> you must not try to climb the ladder of success and power,
> becoming more and more important.
> Instead, you must walk *down* the ladder,
> to meet and walk with people
> who are broken and in pain.
> The light is there, shining in the darkness,
> in the darkness of their poverty.
> The poor with whom you are called to share your life
> and perhaps the sick and the old;
> people out of work,
> young people caught up in the world of drugs,
> people angry because they were terribly hurt when they were young,
> people with disabilities or sick with AIDS,
> or just out of prison;
> people in slums or ghettos,
> people in far-off lands
> where there is much hunger and suffering,
> people who are oppressed
> because of the colour of their skin,
> people who are lonely in overcrowded cities,
> people in pain.[7]

In *Sword and Spirit: Christianity in a Divided World* (BBC/Marshall Pickering, 1989) the political theologian Charles Elliott examined six Christian communities in war-torn and oppressed parts of the world which had found out for themselves just how healing and costly grace is. By meditating on the Gospels these Christians have discovered that God is a God of liberation who wants to set his oppressed people free. Whether they are the slum dwellers of Brazil imprisoned by the poverty created by an oppressive capitalist regime or the Christians of Poland oppressed by the violence of a communist state or the women of America restricted by religious patriarchy, they have come to realize that God is on their side, affirming their dignity both as individuals and as members of a group and calling them to a new free existence. This call brings them into conflict with the oppressive power, conflict that puts their lives and liberty even more at risk, but these people are convinced that God's healing, liberative grace is worth dying for.

Any personal relationship can mediate God's healing grace. Some people find it easier than others to sustain a personal relationship with God through prayer. For those who are not put off by the fact that a great deal of what passes as prayer is not a communion with the God revealed by Christ but a conversation with an idol, usually an ill-disguised portrait of oneself, prayer can be sacramental. For, by meditating upon the human condition before God, we can be made aware of our own brokenness, God's acceptance and the implications of that acceptance. Prayer can, however, become a mere symptom of our brokenness. It is easy to use prayer to try to impose upon God our own desires, concerns and opinions and to justify our alienated condition. We avoid the guilt and frustration of facing our shared responsibility for most of the misery in the world by turning in upon ourselves and concerning ourselves only with our own salvation. When we hear the words "Let us pray" what do most of us do? We bow our heads, close our eyes, perhaps kneel down, and immediately start to think about our own needs and pet causes. We turn in upon ourselves and we set the agenda. We are afraid to let God in in case he shows us something or someone we do not want to see and calls us into situations we would rather avoid. A person who is seeking wholeness and has a desire to communicate God's grace to others will, metaphorically at least, pray with their eyes open, to allow God to direct their eyes towards what forms their shadow side, in need of love and acceptance, and also towards people and situations calling for his healing grace. St Francis of Assisi was a man who knew better than most what the prayer of a recipient of God's grace should be:

> Lord, make me an instrument of your peace,
> Where there is hatred, let me sow love;
> Where there is injury – pardon;
> Where there is doubt – faith;
> Where there is despair – hope;
> Where there is darkness – light;
> And where there is sadness – joy.
> Lord, grant that I may seek rather to comfort
> than to be comforted,

to understand rather than to be understood,
to love than to be loved.
For it is by giving that one receives,
by forgiving that one is forgiven
and by dying that one awakens to eternal life.

The Roman Catholic psychiatrist Jack Dominian has argued that one of the most important functions of marriage is healing. He points out that a person's earliest years are usually full of emotional upheavals that leave deep scars upon the personality. Only a permanent, secure and loving relationship provides the necessary environment for the healing of these emotional scars; it can take a whole lifetime to heal some of the wounds which are repeatedly reopened by events that evoke memories of past hurts and rejection (Jack Dominian, *Marriage, Faith and Love*, Darton, Longman and Todd, 1981). Any relationship based upon love and acceptance can become sacramental, *ubi caritas et amor, Deus ibi est* – where charity and love are found, God himself is there.

Some people's whole lives manifest the grace of God, even though they themselves would not recognize it. They are living testimony to the truth that out of death comes life, out of brokenness, wholeness and out of despair, hope. The Swiss psychologist Paul Tournier believes that love transforms the depravity of individuals into something creative.

> The person matures, develops, becomes more creative, not because of deprivation in itself, but through his own active response to misfortune,

through the struggle to come to terms with it and morally to overcome it . . . Love, one might say, changes the sign of deprivation from minus to plus. Without love, deprivation has a negative coefficient. Love applies a positive coefficient.[8]

People who rise above their own deprivation can become sacraments, mediating wholeness to others who are inspired by their courage and determination. Their lives bear witness to the reality of resurrection that comes after and through death. St Paul put it like this:

> We are afflicted in every way, but not crushed; perplexed, but not driven to despair; persecuted, but not forsaken; struck down, but not destroyed; always carrying in the body the death of Jesus, so that the life of Jesus may also be manifested in our bodies. 2 Corinthians 4:8–10

Human beings are not the only part of God's creation that can be sacramental. The beauty, power and variety of nature, works of art and music have led many to an understanding of the healing nature of God. For many people, especially those alone and isolated, the closest friend they have is not a human being but an animal and animals too can become the mediators of God's grace. It did not matter to me what my own dog did – ignore me, bite me, prefer the company of someone else, refuse to do what he was told. I loved him far too much to be angry with him. One day, when we were sitting watching television together, I realized that just as there were no strings attached to my love for George so there are no strings to God's love for us. This had a profound effect upon me – it healed my constant disabling guilt and fear at being a "sinner" and deserving of God's wrath and set me free to become less preoccupied with myself and more concerned with others.

Any part of God's creation, any person, any situation, any incident negative or positive, can become sacramental, can be used by God to burst in upon our consciousness and reveal his true nature and desire for his creation to be healed and whole. Why then is it that the Church isolates certain rituals and labels them as sacraments?

4

The Sacraments

The Emergence of the Church and Sacraments

"Christ preached the Kingdom of God and the Church appeared." You can almost hear the sigh of disappointment in these famous words of Alfred Loisy the nineteenth-century French theologian (although Loisy himself did not intend to make a negative point). Jesus announced the coming of the kingdom, the complete overturning of the values and structures of the world order, the end of human brokenness and the dawn of the age of wholeness. This was good news for some, for those who were prepared to turn their lives around and live according to the values of the kingdom. But it was bad news to those who were so enslaved to the Law that they could not see their own brokenness and were too afraid to allow God's love made manifest in and through Jesus to free them from enslavement.

Luke tells us that Jesus summed up the nature of the kingdom using the words of Isaiah 61:1–2:

> "The Spirit of the Lord is upon me, because he
> has anointed me to preach good news to the poor.
> He has sent me to proclaim release to the captives

and recovering of sight to the blind, to set at
liberty those who are oppressed, to proclaim the
acceptable year of the Lord." . . . And he began
to say to them, "Today this scripture has been
fulfilled in your hearing." Luke 4:18–21

The centre of the kingdom was love; love that liberates
people from their brokenness and alienation and
enables them to love their neighbour with an
unselfish, active love. The kingdom was to be a *community* characterized by an absence of rules, attitudes
and structures that would alienate people from each
other and lead to the depersonalization and marginalization of some; a community of equality, trust, intimacy and direct contact between members. The kingdom was not only about the individual's relationship
with God, but also about the individual's relationship
with the rest of humanity, about society's treatment
of its members. Jesus did not go around alone giving
individually directed retreats. He gathered together a
small community as a symbol and nucleus of the
coming kingdom. This community included the
twelve men or apostles who represented the twelve
tribes of Israel and symbolized the new Israel, the
new kingdom that Jesus was constituting.

The nucleus community did not keep itself to itself;
it reached out to others, touching the hearts of men
and women and sowing the seeds of the kingdom in
homes, villages and towns. Jesus was the centre of all
this, the channel of the divine love which flowed out
encompassing those who were ready to receive it,
transforming their brokenness into wholeness. It was

Jesus who was the most important and obvious sacrament of God's love. Of course, it was a physical impossibility for Jesus to reach every person in Judaea to alert them to the coming of the kingdom so he trusted in a direct intervention from God to establish the kingdom. Yet it did not come and, dying on the cross, defeated by the power of the civil and religious authorities, rejected by those whom he had healed and loved, it must have seemed to Jesus that his whole life had been a waste of time and effort. Perhaps he had fundamentally misunderstood the nature of God? It must have appeared in those terrible moments that his opponents had been right, that God was a legalist.

However, out of this failure God wrought success and out of Jesus' broken body and spirit he raised a transformed and healed person. The risen Christ was not restricted by the confines of the unrisen human body to one specific place and time. He became available to everyone at all times. The New Testament writers refer to this new state of Christ's being as "Holy Spirit" or, in John's Gospel, the "paraclete" – the advocate. The Holy Spirit continues to bind Jesus' followers together in community and through them continues to prepare the way for the kingdom. It was this community held together by the Spirit that became the Church.

The Greek word *ekklesia* (translated "Church" in our English New Testaments) originally referred to an assembly of people who met together in order to legislate for a city. Only those citizens who possessed full civil rights could participate in the assembly. It had no religious connotations in this context. It is easy to understand why the first Christians adopted this word to describe their community. It conveyed the fact that in the community established by Christ all are equal, there is no hierarchy or rank. In the Greek translation of the Jewish Law the Hebrew word *kahal*, meaning the assembly of the Jewish people, was translated by the word *ekklesia*. Thus by adopting this term the early Christians were emphasizing the fact both that they were something new and radical but also that they were the members of God's chosen people – the "new Israel".

At first the Church seems to have stayed faithful to the values of the kingdom which it proclaimed. The book of Acts tells us that the first Christians "had all things in common; and they sold their possessions and goods and distributed them to all, as any had need" (Acts 2:44–5). Priesthood and hierarchy of any kind were eschewed, all were equal in the community of Christ. As Paul so eloquently put it:

> There is neither Jew nor Greek, there is neither slave nor free, there is neither male nor female; for you are all one in Christ Jesus. Galatians 3:28

The central act of worship was a simple meal at which bread was broken.

The Church did not identify itself with the kingdom of God. The kingdom had still not arrived. The Church's task was to continue Christ's work of preparing the ground for it and to enable as many as possible to experience the wholeness of resurrection, albeit in a partial way, during their earthly life and to prepare them to participate in the resurrection of

118

the dead. The Church came to understand itself as the body of Christ, the community through which God reaches out to the whole world.

As time went on and Christianity spread, much of the original vision and ideals of the earliest Church was lost. A Church order and hierarchy developed that led to a distinction being drawn between those empowered to preside over the liturgy and the people. Eventually women were excluded from the ministry and by the Middle Ages the Church had developed a priestly hierarchy. Gone was the community in which all were equal. After two and a half centuries of being considered a subversive force in the Roman Empire (because Christians would not worship the gods upon whom the stability and well-being of the Empire were thought to depend), under the Emperor Constantine, Christianity became a recognized and respected religion. The Church became part of the world and its values, the establishment of the kingdom of God was no longer a priority.

Belief in Jesus' two-fold nature – divine and human – was the chief concern of the Church by the third century. Belief was the means to salvation, how one behaved and what one did became a secondary concern. Disagreement over belief and ritual split the Church. Every so often, attempts were made to reform and reunite the Church and return it to the ideals and values of the apostolic Church. For example, in the thirteenth century St Francis of Assisi attempted to realign the Church with the poor and outcast. The most famous of these attempted reforms was the Protestant Reformation of the sixteenth century. In the twentieth century the Second Vatican Council (1962–5) tried to reform the Roman Catholic Church on the basis of the early Church and this process continues today. However, the Church as a whole is still far from embodying the values of the kingdom. It remains wealthy while large sections of the world are trapped in poverty, it remains hierarchical and exclusivist in many respects, and in many parts of the world the Church bolsters the establishment rather than taking the side of the downtrodden and broken-hearted. The Church tends to be a club rather than a community. Only in small pockets of the world have Christians managed to return to the ideals of the early Church. These Christians tend to be members of oppressed groups, who, having been largely abandoned by the remote authorities of the Church, have seized the Gospel message for themselves and formed themselves into real communities, base communities as they are known in Latin America, in which the Gospel message of liberation from the forces of brokenness is experienced as a reality. In these communities all are equal, all share everything in common, learn together by studying the Bible and often worship by breaking bread together without priests. These communities stand as symbols of love and human potential in a situation of injustice and oppression.

Even after his death Jesus remained the heart of the Christian community, the source of the love that bound it together, vitalizing it and propelling it outwards to take the love where it was most needed. The early Christians were convinced that Jesus was alive and continuing his work of enabling people to experience wholeness and urging those whom he encountered to work for the establishment of the kingdom. Now there was even better news to proclaim, the news that God had raised him from nothingness into a new healed and whole existence and that he had blazed a trail which all humanity could follow. As the author of the Epistle to Hebrews put it: "Jesus has gone as a forerunner on our behalf" (Hebrews 6:20), all men and women are destined for this salvation.

Since Jesus is the most perfect sign of God's love and sacrament of salvation it was important for people to be able to encounter him in a real, personal and substantial way, even though he could no longer be met in the same way as before his death.

In chapter three we established that because God is the source of all creation and became one with it in Jesus Christ, almost any relationship can become sacramental and mediate God's healing, resurrecting love. As a community, however, there was a need for ways to express the binding together in love of the followers of Christ and to enable all members of the community to share the healing love of Christ. So the early Christians came to believe that, in meeting together and performing symbolic actions particularly associated with the life and work of Christ, they experienced his saving presence with them in a very real way. Therein lay the origins of the Church's liturgy and sacraments.

Many Christians are today highly suspicious of the use of symbolism in worship. They fear a tendency to

treat symbols as if they were the realities they are
supposed to represent, a tendency that can lead to
idolatry. It is, considering the history of the Church,
a justified fear, but not one that should be allowed to
result in the exclusion of all symbolism from worship.
One of the greatest contributions to human self-
understanding was made by the psychologist Carl
Gustav Jung when he pointed out that human beings
deal in symbols all the time:

> What we call a symbol is a term, a name, or even
> a picture that may be familiar in daily life, yet
> that possesses specific connotations in additional
> to its conventional and obvious meaning. It
> implies something vague, unknown, or hidden
> from us ... As the mind explores the symbol, it
> is led to ideas that lie beyond the grasp of
> reason ... Because there are innumerable things
> beyond the range of human understanding, we
> constantly use symbolic terms to represent con-
> cepts that we cannot define or fully comprehend.
> This is one reason why all religions employ sym-
> bolic language or images.[1]

Symbolism is natural to humanity and essential for
its self-understanding.

We use symbols to express feelings and to articulate
realities too deep, complex or mysterious for words.
When we love someone, for example, we kiss them,
we speak the words "I love you" and hold them close
to us, whilst all the time being painfully aware of the
inadequacy of these expressions of our love. We know
that the kiss, the hug, the terms of endearment are

122

not the love itself but simply expressions of it. However, the love would not be complete unless we attempted to express it. Some people confuse the expressions of love with love itself, but this is a distortion. Symbols are there to point the way to a better understanding. As Paul put it, "now we see in a mirror dimly, but then face to face" (1 Corinthians 13:12). Symbols help us to perceive something of things so deep and profound that we can never hope to grasp them completely in this life.

God's love for us, his giving of himself to us and his promise of healing and wholeness, touch upon the very depths of our existence. They are realities so deep, so precious, involving such extreme emotion that they can only be expressed through symbol, through sacrament. God cannot be fully encapsulated in human words or understanding. All God-talk, whether biblical or not, is essentially metaphorical and symbolic. So sacraments should not be feared by Christians as potential obstacles between God and humanity. On the contrary, they are the means through which obstacles can be overcome.

The Church performs the sacraments in the context of its liturgy, as part of its public, communal and ordered gatherings for the purpose of worship. Some people believe that the sacraments should not be celebrated in such an ordered way; they argue that Christians should rely upon the Holy Spirit to direct their worship spontaneously. Yet when we participate in liturgy we are attempting to encounter God. It is impossible to get to know and love someone, to reach down into the depths of their being, if every time you meet them they are totally different and behave unpredictably. So it is with the liturgy in which we attempt to encounter God. Familiar patterns of words and actions should enable us to go deeper into the realities they express. We should not have to spend all our worship time in the uncomfortable state of wondering what is going to happen next. Ordered liturgy supported by symbolism provides us with a safe environment in which we can learn to face aspects of ourselves that in normal circumstances we would try to avoid for fear of destroying ourselves. We focus upon the life and work of one person, Jesus Christ, but we are forced to reflect upon our own lives – his life acts as a judgement on our own. The liturgy provides us with the means and security to bear such reflection and it also enables us to make some sense of the pain and brokenness of our lives.

The Sacrament of Baptism

The sacrament of baptism has its origins in the ritual of Judaism. By the time of Jesus it was customary for Gentile men and women who wished to become proselytes of Judaism to undergo a ritual water bath whereby they were both cleansed from the impurity of Gentile living and initiated into the Jewish faith and way of life. The most famous exponent of baptism was, of course, John the Baptist.

John the baptizer appeared in the wilderness,

preaching a baptism of repentance for the forgiveness of sins. And there went out to him all
the country of Judea, and all the people of Jerusalem; and they were baptized by him in the river
Jordan, confessing their sins. Mark 1:4–5

Like Jesus after him, John was convinced that the
kingdom of God was about to be established. God
was about to intervene in history and it was therefore
necessary to ensure that one was ready, that one had
begun to live the sort of life appropriate to someone
who knew that God had forgiven their sins. John's
baptism was therefore a rite of initiation into the
kingdom of God and a purification. Jesus himself
underwent this baptism (indicating incidentally that
he was under the impression that he was in need of
forgiveness). Some scholars believe that Jesus began
his public ministry as a disciple of John. Whether this
was the case or not, it does seem that Jesus developed
very different ideas about the kingdom. Unlike John,
Jesus appears to have been convinced that the kingdom was open to all and not conditional upon any
ritual; all that was needed was an acknowledgement
of one's own brokenness. The only specific mention
of baptism by Jesus in the Gospels is in Matthew
28:19 where the risen Jesus instructs his followers to
go and make disciples of all nations, baptizing them
in the name of the Father, Son and Holy Spirit. But
most New Testament scholars regard this as a very
early interpolation into the text to justify the Church's
practice of baptism.

The early Church revived the practice of baptism as a means of initiation, initiation into the death and resurrection of Jesus Christ. By the time the earliest books of the New Testament came to be composed a quite sophisticated theology of baptism had already been developed. Paul taught that through baptism people came to share in the death and resurrection of Christ:

> Do you not know that all of us who have been baptized into Christ Jesus were baptized into his death? We were buried therefore with him by baptism into death, so that as Christ was raised from the dead by the glory of the Father, we too might walk in newness of life. For if we have been united with him in a death like his, we shall certainly be united with him in a resurrection like his. Romans 6:3–5

As a consequence Christians were no longer enslaved to the Law and sin but owed allegiance only to Christ and God's grace.

The author of the Epistle to the Hebrews saw baptism as a purification:

> Let us draw near with a true heart in full assurance of faith, with our hearts sprinkled clean from an evil conscience and our bodies washed with pure water. Hebrews 10:22

In Acts, Peter is portrayed as associating baptism with repentance and the forgiveness of sins:

> And Peter said to them, "Repent, and be bap-

tized every one of you in the name of Jesus Christ
for the forgiveness of your sins; and you shall
receive the gift of the Holy Spirit." Acts 2:38

Initially baptism took place in the name of Jesus
Christ to indicate that the person being baptized was
submitting his or herself to the authority of Jesus and
his message. Later on, as the doctrine of the Trinity
developed, baptism was administered in the name of
the Father, Son and Holy Spirit.

We are lucky to have an extant account of baptism
in the early Church in a document known as *The
Didache*, or *The Teaching of the Lord to the Gentiles,
Through the Twelve Apostles*, which is made up of teaching on Christian morality and a manual of rules dealing with various aspects of Church life. It is usually
dated around AD 100–150.

> The procedure for baptism is as follows. After
> rehearsing all the preliminaries, immerse in running water "In the name of the Father, and of
> the Son, and of the Holy Ghost". If no running
> water is available, immerse in ordinary water.
> This should be cold if possible; otherwise warm.
> If neither is practicable, then sprinkle water three
> times on the head "In the name of the Father,
> and of the Son, and of the Holy Ghost". Both
> baptizer and baptized ought to fast before the
> baptism, as well as any others who can do so,
> but the candidate himself should be told to keep
> a fast a day or two beforehand.

Other sources tell us that, as well as fasting, candidates for baptism in the early Church also had to confess their sins and renounce the devil. After baptism the baptizer laid his hands upon the head of the baptized and invoked the Holy Spirit to come upon them. This was followed by the consumption of some milk and honey. In the Old Testament the land promised to Israel by God is often described as "a land flowing with milk and honey", a land that would be sweet to live in because it would nourish the inhabitants. Eating the honey and drinking the milk was therefore a symbolic gesture to convey the conviction that the baptized had entered into the inheritance prepared by God and revealed through Jesus, namely participation in the resurrection and a whole, healed existence.

At first only adults were baptized and it was believed that any sin committed after baptism could not be forgiven. But this belief was soon modified and by the fifth century infant baptisms had become the norm. From the second until the fourth centuries baptisms only took place at Easter and perhaps one other time of year, although exceptions were made for people in danger of death.

It is easy to understand why the early Christians found the already existing Jewish rite of baptism so easy to adapt to reflect their understanding of what God had brought about through Jesus. The immersion (whether literal or symbolically performed by sprinkling) in cold water symbolized death, destruction and annihilation, utter brokenness. In dreams our unconscious, which we often find frightening and threatening, is often represented as water. But water does not only symbolize destruction and chaos, it can be a sign of creation and life. According to Genesis 1:1–9 it was out of the waters of chaos that God brought forth creation. Water is life-giving, cleansing and preserving. The rite of baptism in which the candidate is plunged into running water and then pulled out naturally lent itself to a symbolic representation of the death and resurrection of Christ. The candidate is immersed in the swirling, lethal waters which symbolize the forces of evil, chaos and brokenness. The waters close over the candidate's head, symbolizing the triumph of those forces of destruction over the person. At that moment the person is utterly broken, destroyed completely, the person is dead.

Perhaps at this point it becomes clearer how liturgy provides us with a safe environment in which we can learn to face aspects of ourselves that in normal circumstances we would try to avoid for fear of self-destruction. Back in chapter one we established that we all walk in the face of death and destruction. We are all broken. Yet quite naturally we are afraid to face this for fear that the reality will be too much for us to bear. Baptism like all sacramental liturgy enables us to face these facts by representing them symbolically, so in a sense we are one step removed from them. It is as if our lives are being played out in front of us on a stage or screen. What is portrayed is real and affects us profoundly and yet we are able to view it from a perspective that is safe. The Christian liturgy also enables us to face these awful facts in the light of the resurrection, so that death is always viewed from the perspective of life. This does not make death an easier prospect but means it is a leap of faith, "in sure and certain hope of the Resurrection". When we partake in the liturgy, therefore, we have the opportunity to face the most appalling and difficult realities, realities that we spend the rest of our lives avoiding, because we are safe in the knowledge that every end leads to a beginning.

In baptism, then, we face death and destruction. Not only are we undergoing complete and utter destruction ourselves but we are also participating in the death of Christ. In baptism we hang on the cross with Jesus of Nazareth, we are with him in his suffering, despair and desolation and we fall with him into depths of non-being. With him we are destroyed by being human.

No one baptizes themselves. This is significant. We are influenced by others, dependent upon others and part of a history and society that have an enormous influence upon our formation. We are all responsible for one another and the act of baptism symbolizes that – no one is ever baptized alone. The candidate is surrounded by people watching him or her being plunged into the waters by another. We are responsible for the brokenness and destruction of others and in baptism the community of believers are asked to face up to this and realize that we stand at the foot of the cross of Christ, responsible for his death, and at the foot of millions of other crosses.

However it is also with the help of another person that the candidate is raised up from the waters. Again this is significant. Just as brokenness is not a private, completely self-inflicted condition, so salvation is not an individual concern. It involves other people because it is about being loved and accepted by God and God mediates his love through his creation in general and through our fellow human beings in particular. We become part of the community of salvation – the kingdom. So the candidate is helped up from the waters and is immediately in the midst of persons representing the kingdom of God.

Just as through the plunging into the waters we participate in the *death* of Christ, so in the emergence from the waters we participate in his resurrection. We are with Christ in his victory over brokenness and death and his new transformed existence of wholeness and life. Through participation in the rite of baptism we affirm that this is our destiny, that in the end God will not allow death and brokenness to have victory over us. We too will be raised to a healed and whole existence.

Before the baptism takes place the candidate is asked (or if the candidate is a child, the parents and god-parents are asked to speak on his or her behalf) to renounce Satan and all his works or sin and evil and affirm their belief in God, Christ and the Holy Spirit by saying the Apostles' Creed. The candidate is therefore asked to declare that he or she desires to move from brokenness to wholeness, to turn around and start again. Of course, as we noted in chapter two, no one achieves complete wholeness in this life, to be human is to be broken and it is inevitable that our baptismal vows will be broken many times in our lives. Therefore it is essential that we are given regular opportunities to renew our vows, preferably at Easter, which is the supreme festival of wholeness emerging from brokenness in Christ.

In some traditions salt is placed in the candidate's mouth before baptism. Salt was used in ancient times as a means of purification. It is used in baptism as a sign that the candidate is in a fit mental and spiritual state to undergo incorporation into the death and resurrection of Christ. In the New Testament purity is understood not in terms of cleanliness but as single-ness of intention and purpose, single-mindedness. The candidate for baptism should only have one over-riding intention, to move from brokenness to whole-ness both as individuals and as part of the embryonic kingdom of God. The placing of salt upon the tongue symbolizes the candidate's commitment to this single-mindedness.

After baptism the candidate is sometimes anointed on the head with olive oil. Like water, oil is an ancient symbol and is capable of symbolizing many different things. Generally speaking, it symbolized distinction and blessedness. In the ancient Jewish world guests were anointed with oil as a sign of welcome:

> Thou preparest a table before me in the presence of my enemies; thou anointest my head with oil, my cup overflows. Psalm 23:5

The anointing of the newly baptized is therefore at one level symbolic of God's joy at their incorporation into the community of salvation. By New Testament times oil had become a symbol of healing and wholeness:

> Is there any among you sick? Let him call for the elders of the church, and let them pray over him, anointing him with oil in the name of the Lord.
> James 5:14

So the anointing of the baptized also symbolizes the healing and wholeness which it is their destiny to receive. In the ancient world corpses were anointed with oil. Christ's body was anointed at Bethany in preparation for his death (Mark 14:1–10). The anointing of the baptized therefore also symbolizes death, the death of the old, terminally broken person. Oil is also the symbol of priesthood and kingship in the Old Testament, a sign of selection by God to fulfil his purposes. The baptized are anointed as a sign of their commissioning by God to become sacraments of his presence in the world and builders of his kingdom.

The baptized or their sponsors will often be handed a lighted candle at this point. The candle is an ancient Christian symbol representing the victory of Christ over darkness and death.

> The light shines in the darkness, and the darkness has not overcome it. John 1:5

In the early Church the baptized were dressed in a white robe as a symbol of their cleansing, their new start. White was also the colour of wedding garments. Jesus often likened the kingdom of God to a wedding feast. The baptized's white robe therefore also symbolized their incorporation into the kingdom. Even in those traditions where adult baptism and full immersion are no longer often practised it is still customary for babies to be dressed in white "christening" robes.

If the baptized person is an adult, baptism will usually be followed, in the main traditions, by the laying on of hands by which the person receives the Holy Spirit, following Peter's instructions in Acts 2. This laying on of hands confirms their initiation into the community of salvation and provides them with the strength of the presence of God to persevere in their baptized existence. In the Roman Catholic and Anglican Churches when people are baptized as infants, it has become the custom to postpone the rite of confirmation until such time as the baptized can choose to have themselves confirmed a member of the Church and be anointed once again and renew their baptismal promises. The separation of confirmation from baptism in the case of those who are baptized as infants serves a very important purpose. When a child is approaching puberty she finds herself undergoing enormous changes physically and mentally and can feel bewildered and helpless. Adults often add to the confusion by refusing to recognize the adolescent as either adult or child but expect them to oscillate between the two. Confirmation provides Christian children with an opportunity to consider their changing circumstances, after which the Church accepts their status as adults. At confirmation the Church asks its young members to reaffirm their commitment to Christ, his healing presence and the kingdom. In the Roman Catholic Church candidates are asked to choose a new name – a sign of their new identity as confirmed members of the Church. Confirmation then provides young people with the chance to make an important decision about their lives. They may not yet feel ready to make such a decision, or they may make what others would regard as the wrong decision but God respects their right to do that. He acknowledges them to be full persons. A mockery is made of the whole rite if the young adults go through it under duress.

So far we have examined the rich religious symbolism of baptism but we are all aware of the fact that many of those who take their children along to be baptized are not committed Christians and have no intention of becoming so, nor do they appear to be at all interested in the spiritual development of their children. In an age when it is possible for people to go from birth to death without ever entering a Christian church why is it that so many still want their babies baptized? Baptism is the only ritual available to the majority of people that incorporates the newborn child into the social community. We all have a desperate desire to be accepted and this includes the things and people we cherish. By having our child baptized we are publicly offering it to our community for acceptance. We formally name it, giving it an identity, and we choose members of the community to be its guardians. Even the most supposedly unreligious of people can still be aware of the threat of brokenness and death, an awareness that can be heightened by the birth of a new and vulnerable person. The Christian ethos of our society, although diminishing, is still great enough for people to perceive that baptism offers some sort of assurance that all will be well. The desire to be assured that ultimately "all will be well" for their child is overwhelmingly strong in most parents and baptism provides a means of expressing that desire and receiving assurance.

Robin Green in his superb book *Only Connect: Worship and Liturgy from the Perspective of Pastoral Care* (Darton, Longman and Todd, 1987) has noted that many parents have mixed feelings about their newborn child; they may at times love him and want to ensure that all will be well but at other times they may hate the child with a frightening, violent intensity. These negative feelings towards the child may dominate in mothers suffering from post-natal depression, in single parents having to cope with a child on their own, in families living in difficult economic and social circumstances, or even in any parent whose child is going through a stage of continuous crying. Green believes that for some parents the rite of baptism, in which the child is symbolically submitted to the powers of violence and death before being raised to new life, provides a valuable and non-destructive ritual through which they may, perhaps unconsciously, come to terms with their ambiguous or unambiguously negative feelings towards their child. The sacrament of baptism, then, is meaningful and important not just to those who are conscious of what God has achieved in Christ; it can be equally significant and vital to those on the margins of Christianity.

Over the years there has been much debate as to

the value and appropriateness of infant baptism. Some would argue that since baptism involves the decision to renounce the path of brokenness and opt for the difficult, crucifying path of wholeness, it is inappropriate for baptism to be offered to newborn babies who are incapable of making any real decisions. Others would want to state that the parent has no right to incorporate the child into the Church and to make vows on behalf of the child – the child has the right to make up its own mind about Christianity when it is old enough to do so.

However baptism is not just about making the important decision to align oneself with Christ. It is about being initiated into a community through which one can tangibly encounter God's love and healing. A parent who would want to postpone initiating a child would be acting with the same illogicality as if they refused to love the child until it was able to respond to their love. As Father Rod Strange has pointed out:

> We do not regard parents' love as an undue pressure likely to handicap a child's growth, nor even as an optional extra. On the contrary, we look sadly on those who have been orphaned because we know they have been deprived of something immensely valuable for their development as whole human beings. By baptism we are ushered into the known realm of God's love. If it has been experienced as a source of pressure – which has too often happened – then that is a tragedy. God loves all that he has made. He loves

137

everyone, Christian and non-Christian, believer
and unbeliever. We cannot escape his love. We
may reject it, but he will never cease to love us.
However, those who have been baptized have
been privileged to have that love made manifest
to them in particular words and through particular signs.[2]

By having their babies baptized parents are simply
demonstrating to the child and to those around them
that God loves the child. Baptism could be said to be
the first divine hug a child receives. The parents and
godparents do make decisions on behalf of the child in
faith but, in later life, confirmation or other occasions
which require the renewal of baptismal vows will provide the child with the opportunity of affirming or
rejecting their baptism.

Baptism is the sacrament of liberation, liberation from
ultimate brokenness and annihilation. Just as God led
his people Israel through the threatening Red Sea
from slavery to liberty, so through the waters of baptism he leads his people from death to life, from brokenness to wholeness. Liberation brings with it
responsibility to work for the liberation of others and
by baptism we are committed to work for the establishment of the kingdom, by being incorporated into
the Church whose purpose is to prepare the way for
the kingdom. As well as being the sacrament of incorporation, baptism is also the sacrament of unity
amongst Christians. Even though Christians are divided and the Church torn apart over matters of doc-

trine and practice, it is the common experience of baptism that establishes the imperfect community that already exists in Christianity and demands that the Church work towards full and unimpaired community.

The Sacrament of the Eucharist

> For I received from the Lord what I also delivered to you, that the Lord Jesus on the night when he was betrayed took bread, and when he had given thanks, he broke it, and said, "This is my body which is for you. Do this in remembrance of me." In the same way also the cup, after supper, saying, "This cup is the new covenant in my blood. Do this, as often as you drink it, in remembrance of me." For as often as you eat this bread and drink the cup, you proclaim the Lord's death until he comes.
>
> 1 Corinthians 11:23–6

We have already observed that one of the most distinguishing features of Jesus' ministry was that he ate and drank with his disciples and those in need of healing love, as a sign of the intimacy and acceptance God offered humankind. By doing so he established and strengthened the community that formed around him. One particular meal that he shared with his disciples came to have great significance for the early Church. This was the last meal that they shared together – the "last supper". The writers of the synoptic

Gospels suggest that this meal was a Passover meal; John implies that it was the meal eaten on the night before Passover.

The Jewish festival of Passover or Pesach celebrates the Exodus of the people of Israel from the land of Egypt where they had been reduced to the status of slaves. On the first night of the Passover the Seder meal is eaten. Every piece of food eaten in this meal has symbolic significance recalling the bitter experience of slavery and the sweetness of liberty. The four cups of wine that are blessed and drunk symbolize joy and the matzah (unleavened bread) is eaten to recall the fact that God called his people out of Egypt so suddenly that they did not have time to let the bread rise. For the Jews the Seder is not merely a commemorative meal. By eating and drinking things that have deep symbolic meaning the Jews believe that in some real sense they are *partaking* in the original Passover. The German philosopher Martin Heidegger pointed out that some events in history, although they constitute a once-and-for-all historical event, are also creative to those who make them part of their history, they become "authentic, repeatable possibilities" and occur again and again in a very real way in their lives, presenting them with new possibilities of existence. The Passover event is an authentic, repeatable possibility for the Jews; so also is the Last Supper for Christians.

It is a matter of debate amongst scholars as to whether Jesus himself reinterpreted the significance of the Passover meal to refer to his own atoning death or whether it was his disciples who came to interpret it that way in the light of his death and resurrection. What is certain is that after Jesus' death his disciples continued to meet together to share a meal (or "love-feast") and to break bread as an act of remembrance of what Jesus had gone through and achieved for them. Just as the Passover was much more than a memorial meal, the breaking of the bread not only recalled what Jesus had done but in some very real way made Jesus truly present to those participating in the meal and was another means by which they were incorporated into his saving death and resurrection. Paul makes this quite clear in his first letter to the Corinthians:

> The cup of blessing which we bless, is it not a participation in the blood of Christ? The bread which we break, is it not a participation in the body of Christ? Because there is one bread, we who are many are one body, for we all partake of the one bread. 1 Corinthians 10:16–17

Not only did participation in the shared meal bring those involved into communion with Jesus Christ, it also brought them into communion with their fellow Christians. True community was established.

Within this simple meal of fellowship lie the origins of the eucharist ("thanksgiving") as we know it today. During the second and third centuries after Christ, as the number of Christians grew, the meal was replaced by a much more structured form of worship. Local Christians gathered together in one place, passages from the law and prophets were read (a practice taken over from the synagogue) as were the memoirs of the apostles. Prayers followed, after which the unbaptized left. The eucharist proper then began with the kiss of peace – a practice common in Judaism which symbolized and sealed the wholeness, the *shalom* of the community. Then bread and wine were presented to the person presiding who offered the eucharistic prayer in which the bread and wine were, in the words of the second-century apologist Justin Martyr, "eucharistized" or consecrated

> by the formula of prayer which comes from Him, and from which our flesh and blood are nourished by transformation in the flesh and blood of that incarnate Jesus.[3]

Then the bread and wine were distributed to all present and some taken to the sick. The basic structure is still reflected in the Mass or communion service of all the main Christian denominations.

How does the eucharist mediate the healing presence of Christ to us today?

The eucharist is recognized as a sacrament by all the major Christian denominations. There is a saying that the Church is never more truly itself than when it celebrates the eucharist. In one sense, to celebrate the eucharist is what the Church is for: in it the people of God remember, give thanks for and participate in the saving life and death of Christ.

I think we can avoid stumbling around the vexed and aged debate of exactly *how* Christ is present in the eucharist by simply acknowledging an important but often overlooked fact. No Christian would want to claim that Christ is absent from the eucharist, nor would any Christian assert that the eucharist is just the acting out of a Bible story. All would want to say that Christ is present in some real way in the eucharist.

In the celebration of the eucharist we remember Christ's healing life and death, but by participating in it we too go through death and come to wholeness. All of us come to the eucharist as broken, battered individuals and as members of a torn and fragmented society. As such, we all stand before the altar or eucharistic table equal before God: woman and man; child and adult; priest and lay person; rich and poor; heterosexual and homosexual; married, divorced or single person; criminals and victims; healthy and sick. All are equally loved by God and destined for wholeness. This is what the eucharist *should* make clear but how can it if it is celebrated in a hierarchical and exclusive way? Traditional churches can be such unwelcoming places – as indeed can the new house churches – they can be insular and give the impression of exclusiveness. Once inside a church, a line of pews can also lead to a situation where "saints" seat themselves at the front and "sinners" skulk near the back. The fact that in many churches all those on the altar or presiding over the celebration of the eucharist will be male and the language used in prayer and worship dominated by masculine terms (e.g. brethren) cannot but serve to undermine the proclamation that before God there is no male and female. The eucharist may be the only time in our lives when we do stand equal with others. The layout and atmosphere of the church should make that equality obvious.

On some occasions we will be more aware of our brokenness than on others but part of the function of the eucharist is to help us to face up to our brokenness both as individuals and as part of a society. This is why one of the first acts we are required to perform in the eucharist is to acknowledge and confess our sins and accept forgiveness. We acknowledge our brokenness and allow Christ to forgive us, to accept and love us as we are. In this act we try to be ourselves, to be honest before God. We concluded earlier that acknowledgement of brokenness is the first step towards wholeness. This is why the early Christians were told to "confess your sins to one another, and pray for one another, that you may be healed" (James 5:16).

Some traditions have developed a separate sacrament, the sacrament of penance or reconciliation (or as it is more commonly known "confession") in order that individuals can acknowledge their own brokenness and experience God's love and forgiveness in an intense and private manner. But there is still a need for us to face up to our responsibility for the brokenness of society and of the world at large – our corporate guilt for the ills of the world. The general confession of sins at the commencement of the eucharist provides an excellent opportunity for those participating to acknowledge shared responsibility for the brokenness of others and to hear the words of forgiveness. We noted earlier that often acknowledgement of brokenness only comes after forgiveness and leads to action or repentance. It is very important therefore that those who participate in the transforming eucharist first be brought to realize their brokenness and know that God wants to set them free to be who they are. Realization of this liberation prompts the congregation to give thanks to God for his saving activity by saying or singing the Gloria.

By choosing to participate in the eucharist we affirm ourselves to be part of the people of God, a divided, broken and yet corporate entity. During the eucharist we listen to readings from the Scriptures: the Old Testament, Psalms, New Testament Epistles and Gospels. When we listen to these passages we are listening to the story of those who have gone before us in the journey of faith and salvation, who have experienced the same failure, despair, and suffering as us and yet have triumphed and been made whole by God's grace. These are healing memories for they should encourage us who are so broken and stumbling to have faith and hope in our salvation. Most importantly we listen to the Gospel – the story of Christ and his healing ministry, death and resurrection to wholeness – believing that his story is somehow also our story because we have been incorporated into it through baptism.

After a meditation upon the readings in the form of a sermon the congregation remind themselves of what they have been given through baptism by reciting the creed and then the prayers of intercession are said. So often such prayers can turn into ill-disguised attempts to control God and to dictate his actions. But the God revealed by Christ is not a cosmic Santa

Claus ready to grant our wishes if we promise to be good or say the right sort of thing. The God revealed by Jesus is a God who is able to transform suffering into joy and brokenness into wholeness. Prayer then should focus on the brokenness around us and take the form of a commitment to co-operate with the purposes of God in bringing wholeness and salvation. In the case of incidents where salvation seems an impossibility, all one can do is stand before God in silent trust, resting in his ability and desire to raise order from chaos, even if at present we cannot perceive how that is going to be possible.

After the prayers, the offertory usually takes place. The bread and wine are taken through the congregation and presented to the celebrant. Bread and wine were both such ordinary, everyday things in Jesus' time, like tea and biscuits in our own day. Ordinary, dispensable and easily broken – just like you and I. God chooses to make himself available to humanity in ordinary fragile things. He is in the bread and wine and so are we; they focus as a fusing point of our common humanity. The bread and wine are then consecrated using the words spoken by Jesus during his last supper. The bread is broken and the wine poured out. We break that bread symbolic of his body and his self, and our body, our selves.

Coming face to face with our brokenness represented in such a vivid way as the tearing of a piece of bread or the cracking of a host can be an extremely painful experience. Illusions are shattered as we realize that, both as individuals and as a society, we are not "OK", "all right", "bearing up" or "managing".

On the contrary, we are defeated and broken by life. But, as Bonhoeffer reminded us, grace is not cheap, it cannot be collected simply by visiting a church and participating in the sacraments as a passive observer. Grace was and is costly, involving pain and death. Augustine said something very similar many centuries before:

> If you wish to understand the body of Christ, listen to the apostle telling the faithful: You are the body of Christ and its members. If therefore you are the body of Christ and its members, it is the sacrament of you yourselves that reposes on the table of the Lord: you receive the sacrament of you yourselves. To that which you are you respond by saying Amen, and in that response you assent to it. Be a member of the body of Christ, so that your Amen might be sincere.[4]

In the eucharist we suffer with Christ. Yet, all the time (in most traditions) candles burn upon the altar as a sign that God illuminated the darkness with love and that resurrection and wholeness follow death and brokenness. The eucharist, like baptism, is a "safe" environment in which to face ourselves and our broken state because we face the brokenness in the context of the story of salvation.

Either before or after the consecration the congregation exchange the sign of peace. Robin Green explains the significance of this act:

> The Peace sets our personal pain within a social context of reconciliation: the reconciliation of the

whole created order and the whole of humanity
to God. It offers release from the oppressions
that damage us as a people and challenges the
contemporary political heresies that human
beings are only to be valued for what they own
and possess . . . When human beings worship,
their true self is restored to them individually
and socially. Worship is, therefore, an end in
itself and by its very nature the most radical
critique of every political ideology.[5]

The sign of peace is a sign of the kingdom, a foretaste
of the *shalom* – the personal and societal wholeness
that will be the essence of the kingdom of God. The
eucharist is in a real sense a dangerous, politically
subversive sacrament because when we participate in
it we stand for a few brief moments in the kingdom,
in wholeness, and this should awaken in us an awareness of how far the rest of the world is from the
kingdom and should sharpen our desire to transform
our broken world. The eucharist creates true society
and in this sense is the most revolutionary act one
can participate in.

After the consecration we eat and drink of the bread
and wine as a sign of our desire as individuals and as
Church to participate in the death and life of Christ,
and as an acknowledgement that we believe that we
are *on our way* to wholeness. You will remember that
I cannot agree with those Christians who take a
"wham-bam" attitude to God's saving activity in
them (that it happens, it is an individual matter, it is
perfect and "I am saved"). We are certainly all des-

tined in God's love for wholeness but the process of healing, which involves all of society as well as individuals, is long and hard and can never be fully accomplished in this life.

The eucharist is the only sacrament that most Christians participate in regularly. It is therefore a vital means of mediating God's healing grace to his people. The problem is that in all denominations the eucharist is usually not celebrated in such a way as to bring out its healing character. As I said earlier, the eucharist should be celebrated in a way that draws attention to the equality of all before God. Perhaps this can only come about when, like the base communities in Latin America, the eucharist is celebrated by all the congregation gathered around the altar, with no one presiding over anyone else. There should be plenty of periods of silence in the eucharist in which people can be themselves before God with their own concerns and preoccupations and meditate upon what it is that they are participating in. The eucharist should never be rushed. It should be performed with reverence and dignity; the reality must be given the chance to be conveyed by the symbol. This does not mean that it should be dull nor unnecessarily solemn or traditional, but it does mean that the eucharist like all liturgy should be predictable. A totally unstructured eucharist is unlikely to help the occasional worshipper who might be in great need of the healing it mediates.

Many people come to the eucharist angry: angry with God, with themselves, with others, with society and with the Church. Acknowledgement of anger and bitterness is essential to any healing process, yet unlike their Jewish predecessors, Christians have never been very good at admitting their anger and disappointment with God and there is no place for such vital expression in any of the forms of eucharist used by the major denominations.

Much more serious than this, however, is the way in which the Church has turned the eucharist into an exclusive dining club to which the marginalized and despised are not invited. In some denominations the unbaptized, members of other denominations, divorcees who have remarried, practising homosexuals, those who have had abortions, and others, are all barred from receiving the bread and wine. On the question of intercommunion many would say that since the eucharist is the sacrament of unity it is inappropriate for Christians to celebrate it together until unity is achieved. On the other hand, however, if the eucharist is the sacrament of unity, how can the Church ever hope to reach the state of full communion if Christians do not approach the altar together to acknowledge their guilt for the divisions and to receive the grace of God which will enable them to heal their schisms? As James Mackey has argued:

> since the Eucharist is the primordial embodiment of the spirit of Jesus in the world it is to the Eucharist that Christians, all Christians, must first go in order to have that spirit in them which is also in Christ Jesus. Any "officer" who prevents Christians from participating in a Eucharist celebrated by another Christian church, . . . is actively propounding a false view of

Christianity . . . if the Eucharist is the primary embodiment of the power and presence of Jesus in the world and if the Christian community is the celebrant of the Eucharist, then it is primarily the responsibility of the Christian community-at-large to break bread together in any and every local church which the community can recognize to be celebrating a true sacrament of unity in the spirit of Jesus.[6]

To refuse anyone participation in the sacramental remembrance of God's salvation or healing is blasphemous. It undermines everything that Christ taught: that God loves all unconditionally and has a particular concern for those disregarded or hated – not in order to reform them in the sense of making them conform to the expectations of others but because they need particular assurance of God's love and promise of wholeness. The Church is never less the body of Christ than when it refuses the eucharist to anyone.

5

Conclusion

The Future of Sacraments

Most Christians would accept that baptism and the eucharist are sacraments of God's healing grace. The Roman Catholic and Orthodox Churches, however, hold that there are seven sacraments. These are, in addition to those just discussed: Reconciliation (or Penance); Confirmation; Marriage; Holy Orders and the Sacrament of the Sick (or Extreme Unction). The Anglican Church regards these five as "lesser" sacraments. What is obvious is that most of these seven sacraments constitute rites of passage, that is to say, most are celebrated when a person is moving from one clearly defined stage in life to another. Baptism usually occurs shortly after birth, the child is named and initiated into society. Even if baptism takes place as an adult it signifies the transition a person has made from unbelief or lack of commitment into committed faith. Confirmation is usually celebrated around the time of puberty when the child is going through the painful transition into adulthood. Marriage constitutes another rite of passage from being a single person and part of one family into a couple and new family group. Through the sacrament of ordination people dedicate the rest of their lives to the service of God and the Church in a very particular way. The celebration of the sacrament of the sick is to enable a person to make the often painful and distressing journey from this life through death to wholeness fortified by the assurance of God's love.

The development of these seven sacraments reveals something very important – that people feel the need to experience God's healing grace in a tangible and specific way at times when their lives are going through a process of transformation and they are going through the turbulence and confusion that endings and new beginnings always bring. Participation in the sacraments and identification with the progression of Christ from broken human being into a new healed, whole existence enables or helps a person come to terms with their hopes, regrets, fears and doubts and gives them the strength to step into the unknown of the future, trusting in the healing presence of Christ.

The number of sacraments was fixed in the fifteenth century. We live on the verge of the twenty-first century and experience common processes of transformation that our ancestors did not. Our understanding of the sort of God we are dealing with is very different from that of medieval Christianity; we no longer think of God mainly as king, ruler, judge; we have discovered the suffering, crucified God who does not rule above humanity but travels along with it, a God who is not overwhelmingly masculine. The time is ripe for the development of new sacramental and symbolic rites of passage to represent God's work of salvation in a way that will speak to and answer the needs of modern men and women. All rites of passage involve dying and rising, leaving behind certain things, people and parts of ourselves, and moving on to a new life, new relationships and a new understanding of ourselves. It is therefore particularly important that they be celebrated in a sacramental manner. Let me just give a few pointers to explain what I mean.

In our day one in three marriages ends in divorce. Many of these marriages will have been celebrated in churches by people who were committed to each other and their vows. Marriages break down for a great many complicated reasons but the process is always traumatic for those involved, however "civilized" the relationship between partners. For those going through a divorce one of the most difficult things to cope with is the fact that there is no point, apart from court, at which the marriage can be declared at an end before society. There is no point at which the couple can stand together in front of the family and friends who have been part of their relationship and say to them and each other: "This is the end, we both have to begin again but I want to thank you for your love, our children and the good times we had together and I ask forgiveness for the pain and hurt I have caused you". Very many divorced couples regret that there is no ritual to help them, their children and friends come to terms with the end of one stage of their lives and a new beginning. We need to tie up loose ends, we need to face up to failure in order to be able to start again and we need the witness and support of those closest to us. Many also need the strength of God's healing grace at such a time. They need to know that God is not a judge in a divorce court, he does not apportion blame, he doesn't condemn, he simply loves unconditionally and his love can heal. Those who are going through a divorce are generally traumatized, hurt, vulnerable and frightened people – just the sort of people Jesus reached out to and the Church as his body on earth should respond to their needs and develop a sacrament appropriate to their passage.

Redundancy or retirement can also be traumatic events for some. Feelings of rejection, uselessness, loneliness, fear of old age or of a life without purpose can eat away at a person. Once again, an appropriate sacramental rite could help a person come to terms with the transformation. Creative use of symbols both for work and for periods of rest or retirement could result in a moving, life-giving ritual which would enable the person to go forward into the new stage of their lives backed up with the love of God and friends.

Coming to terms with the loss of a loved one through death is a particularly painful process. In some traditions the funeral service always takes the form of a eucharist and this is very important because there are few times in one's life when one feels the intense need of God's presence more than when one is faced with the death of someone you loved and cherished. However, the problem with celebrating the eucharist at a funeral (as indeed at a wedding) is that some Christians will not be welcome or not feel able to participate in the eucharist celebrated by Christians of other traditions, so that at the very time when people want to feel united and close to one another and God they are divided. In some cases of bereavement no rite is available and here the Church has shamefully failed in its mission to take Christ to those who need him. Those who have lost a child through miscarriage or abortion, and their family and friends, often feel an intense need to express grief, anger, despair and loss, and acknowledge the existence of the child. There is an urgent need for Christians to develop sacramental rites for such situations.

Jesus went to those outcast from society, those whom others dismissed and were afraid of. He loved them and by his love and acceptance challenged the rest of society to do the same. In our society there are many who live on the edges, who want to reintegrate into the community but are prevented from doing so by the attitude of others: prisoners, the homeless, addicts, those who have spent years in hospital, the physically and mentally handicapped, those whose minds have been broken by life. The Church needs to develop sacramental rites that would welcome these people back into society, assure them of their worth in God's sight and pledge practical support and love. Not only would this rite assist the passage of the people involved, it would also be a public call to society to recognize them as full people and care for them. The sacraments enable the Church to be what it is called to be – the means through which Christ continues his work on earth. Christ went to the people, understood their needs and responded accordingly. If the Church is to continue this work then it needs to renew constantly its sacramental rites, making sure that God's love is always available to those who most desperately need it.

NOTES

Introduction

1 Catechism, *The Book of Common Prayer*, 1662

1 Broken Humanity

1 Harry Williams, *Some Day I'll Find You*, Collins Fount, 1984, p. 131
2 Martin Israel, *Healing as Sacrament: The Sanctification of the World*, Darton Longman and Todd, 1984, p. 54
3 Jean Vanier, *The Broken Body: Journey to Wholeness*, Darton Longman and Todd, 1988, p. 1
4 Sheila Cassidy, *Sharing the Darkness: The Spirituality of Caring*, Darton Longman and Todd, 1988, p. 43
5 Norman Autton, *Pain: An Exploration*, Darton Longman and Todd, 1986, p. 107

2 Jesus Christ: the Healer of Brokenness

1 Frank Lake, *Clinical Theology: A Theological and Psychiatric Basis to Pastoral Care*, Darton Longman and Todd, 1966, p. 41
2 Jürgen Moltmann, *The Crucified God*, SCM Press, 1974, pp. 222–3
3 Ibid., p. 203
4 Jean Vanier, *The Broken Body*, p. 106

5 Cited in John Ferguson, *The Place of Suffering*, James Clarke & Son Ltd, 1972, p. 99

3 Transforming Grace

1 Jean Vanier, *The Broken Body*, p. 60
2 Richard P. McBrien, *Catholicism*, Vol. 1, Geoffrey Chapman, 1980, p. 158
3 Richard P. McBrien, *Catholicism*, Vol. 2, p. 732
4 C. S. Lewis, *The Problem of Pain*, Geoffrey Bles, 1940 and Collins Fount, 1957, p. 158
5 Harry Williams, *Tensions: Necessary Conflicts in Life and Love*, Collins Fount, 1989, p. 118
6 Dietrich Bonhoeffer, *The Cost of Discipleship*, trs. Reginald Fuller, SCM Press, 1949
7 Jean Vanier, *The Broken Body*, pp. 72–3
8 Paul Tournier, *Creative Suffering*, SCM Press, 1982, pp. 28–34

4 The Sacraments

1 Carl Jung (ed.), *Man and his Symbols*, Picador, 1978, pp. 3–4
2 Roderick Strange, *The Catholic Faith*, OUP, 1986, p. 87
3 Justin Martyr, *First Apology*, 65 (from R. C. D. Jasper and G. J. Cuming, *The Prayers of the Eucharist Early and Reformed*, Pueblo, 1987, p. 28)
4 St Augustine, *Sermones* 272, cited in Boniface Ramsey, *Beginning to read the Fathers*, Darton Longman and Todd, 1986, p. 103
5 Robin Green, *Only Connect: Worship and Liturgy from the Perspective of Pastoral Care*, Darton Longman and Todd, 1987, p. 45
6 James P. Mackey, *Modern Theology: A Sense of Direction*, OUP, 1987, pp. 152–4